全国高等院校法律英语专业统编教材
法律英语证书（LEC）全国统一考试指定用书

法律英语
视听说

Legal English
Video-Aural-Oral Course

张法连　主编

北京大学出版社
PEKING UNIVERSITY PRESS

图书在版编目(CIP)数据

法律英语视听说 / 张法连主编. —北京:北京大学出版社,2017.9
(全国高等院校法律英语专业统编教材)
ISBN 978-7-301-28668-5

Ⅰ.①法… Ⅱ.①张… Ⅲ.①法律—英语—听说教学—高等学校—教材 Ⅳ.①D9

中国版本图书馆CIP数据核字(2017)第203588号

书　　名	法律英语视听说 FALÜ YINGYU SHI-TING-SHUO
著作责任者	张法连　主编
责任编辑	刘　爽
标准书号	ISBN 978-7-301-28668-5
出版发行	北京大学出版社
地　　址	北京市海淀区成府路205号　100871
网　　址	http://www.pup.cn　新浪微博:@北京大学出版社
电子信箱	nkliushuang@hotmail.com
电　　话	邮购部 62752015　发行部 62750672　编辑部 62759634
印 刷 者	北京圣夫亚美印刷有限公司
经 销 者	新华书店
	787毫米×1092毫米　16开本　16.75印张　350千字 2017年9月第1版　2021年12月第4次印刷
定　　价	49.00元

未经许可,不得以任何方式复制或抄袭本书之部分或全部内容。
版权所有,侵权必究
举报电话:010-62752024　电子信箱: fd@pup.pku.edu.cn
图书如有印装质量问题,请与出版部联系,电话:010-62756370

前言

  在世界经济一体化进程不断加快的时代背景下，我国在国际舞台愈发彰显出国际交流合作的魄力和决心。目前，涉外法务活动空前频繁，法律英语的重要性日益凸显。掌握专业英语已经成为现代法律人必备的职业素质。法律英语作为特殊用途英语（ESP），其学习获得和水平测试与普通英语存在着较大差别。即便对英语为母语的人群来说，法律英语也可谓极其复杂。广大法学学生和法律从业者对法律英语的学习热情空前高涨。然而可惜的是，国内一直没有一个科学的考核指标衡量法律从业人员专业英语的掌握程度。法律英语证书（LEC）全国统一考试的推出为我国法律英语的教与学指明了方向，意义重大，影响深远。

  作为一本专门针对法律英语的视听说教材，本书在选材上注重系统、新颖，材料主要来源于英美等国法学院讲授课例、专题讲座、外媒主流新闻报道、法院文件和少部分律政影视作品；主要涉及了美国宪法、三权分立、英美法法院划分、国际商法、知识产权法、证券法、竞争法、侵权法、合同法、刑法、刑事诉讼程序等相关知识点，涵盖英美法背景知识介绍，能够在训练视听说的同时，充分输入英美法基础知识；并且在训练听力的同时也相应安排了口语练习，相辅相成，能够提高学生的专业表达能力和涉外法律实务技能；本书同时配有案例分析和判决书赏析，以情景模拟的方式让学生浸入式学习法律英语。

  本套教材共包括《法律英语精读教程》（上、下）、《法律英语泛读教程》（上、下）、《法律英语写作教程》《法律英语翻译教程》《英美法律文化教程》《法律英语视听说》《大学法律英语》《基础法律英语》以及配套学习使用的《英美法律术语双解》。

参加本书编写的有：中央司法警官学院刘新凯（1-7课），中国石油大学（华东）刘媛媛（8-14课），湖南涉外经济学院钟玲俐（15-21课），西南政法大学孙林（22-30课）及中国政法大学田力男教授，其中孙林担任了全书的整理和统筹工作，在此谨对各位老师表示诚挚谢意。

各位教师或同学在使用本书的过程中有什么问题，欢迎及时与出版社或编者联系：zhangbook16@163.com。本书免费提供音频、视频材料，请登陆 http://www.pup.cn/，点击下载专区自行下载。

编　者

2017年3月于中国政法大学

目 录

Lesson 1	History of American Law ···································· 1
Lesson 2	Fundamental Doctrine: Stare Decisis Doctrine ············ 7
Lesson 3	Sources of Law (1) ·· 13
Lesson 4	Sources of Law (2) ·· 19
Lesson 5	Comparison of Laws ·· 25
Lesson 6	Types of Legal Actions ······································· 32
Lesson 7	Legal Procedures ·· 40
Lesson 8	American Constitution—State and Federal Conflict ······ 45
Lesson 9	Legal Concepts (1): Bill of Rights (US) ···················· 52
Lesson 10	Legal Concepts (2): Equal Rights ·························· 58
Lesson 11	Legal Concepts (3): Constitutional Crisis ················· 66
Lesson 12	Legal Concepts (4): Presumed Innocent ·················· 74
Lesson 13	Laying Down the Law—English Common Law ············ 81
Lesson 14	The Pursuit of Liberty—English Common Law ··········· 88
Lesson 15	International Business Law ·································· 93
Lesson 16	Business Organization Law ································· 99
Lesson 17	International Commercial Arbitration ····················· 105
Lesson 18	The Dispute Settlement System of WTO ················ 110

Lesson 19	International Center for Settlement of Investment Disputes	116
Lesson 20	Protection of Intellectual Property	121
Lesson 21	United Nations Convention on Contracts for the International Sale of Goods	127
Lesson 22	Economic Law and Types of Property	133
Lesson 23	Laws and Acts of Security	139
Lesson 24	Business Law: Consumer Protection and Product Liability	145
Lesson 25	Law of Contract (1): Basic Principles	150
Lesson 26	Law of Contract (2): Breach and Remedies	156
Lesson 27	Antitrust Law and Sherman Act	161
Lesson 28	Types and Laws of Competition	167
Lesson 29	Criminal Law (1): Basic Principles	172
Lesson 30	Criminal Law (2): Plea Bargaining and Cross Examination	177
Answers		183

Lesson 1
HISTORY OF AMERICAN LAW

Part I Getting Ready

The following words and phrases will appear in this unit. Use five minutes to find out the meanings of these words and phrases.

Listen carefully and study them.

1. Source
2. Legitimate
3. Supreme Court
4. Binding
5. Common law
6. Judicial
7. Constitution
8. Senate
9. House of Representatives
10. Guilty

Part II Overview

The History of American Law

A. Watch the video and answer the following questions.

1. When we want to define a legal term, what can we do?

   _____

   _____

2. When has *Black's Law Dictionary* been published?

   _____

   _____

3. What is the definition of law in *Black's Law Dictionary*?

   _____

   _____

B. Watch the video and decide whether the following statements are true or false.

[ ] 1. *Black's Law Dictionary* plays the final controlling role in defining legal terms.

[ ] 2. The United States Supreme Court states a definition of law through the case of United States Fidelity and Guaranty Co. v. Guenther.

[ ] 3. Laws are designed so that they typically reflect what the minority of the people feel is just or right.

Lesson 1
History of American Law

C. Watch the video and fill in the blanks.

People make law, and it is made to reflect how the people feel about certain actions or conduct, such as (1)_____, (2)_____ or (3)_____. There is a purposeful and strong connection between law and that (4)_____. This is a theme you will see often in (5)_____ and also throughout all other areas of the law.

D. Watch the video and answer the following questions.

1. Where did American law system come from?

   _____
   _____

2. What is the English common law rooted in?

   _____
   _____

3. Much of the common law was formed in the years between the Norman Conquest of England in the early 11th century and the settlement of the American colonies in the early 17th century, wasn't it?

   _____
   _____

E. Watch the video and answer the following questions.

1. When did Sir William Blackstone publish *Commentaries on the Laws of England* as a complete overview of the English common law?

   _____
   _____

2. How many volumes did Blackstone's *Commentaries* span?

   _____
   _____

3. What are judicial decisions?

   _____

   _____

4. Why did American Founding Fathers adopt this system of common law?

   _____

   _____

Part III Further Understanding

A. Watch the video and fill in the blanks.

The English (1)_____ is based on a cultural system of (2)_____ through local custom. The early tribes of England each held their own set of customs, but this system became (3)_____ as those early tribal peoples came (4)_____. These ancient customs are the (5)_____ that eventually became part of the American system of justice.

B. (a) Watch the video and decide whether the following statements are true or false.

[ ] 1. The decision-maker in England can decide cases without using established guidelines and traditions.

[ ] 2. By carrying forward and preserving these customs, the courts assured that the law was truly "common" to all.

Lesson 1
History of American Law

(b) Choose the best answer for each question.

1. When Smith, Jones' neighbor, inadvertently builds his barn on Jones' land, which claim will the court support?

    A. Jones claims ownership of the barn.

    B. Smith claims ownership of the barn.

    C. Smith claims that he owns that small portion of land the barn occupies.

    D. Both B and C.

2. What is the main purpose through that case ?

    A. Remind people that they cannot build fixtures on others' land.

    B. Remind all landowners that they must be careful not to allow others to build permanent fixtures on their land.

    C. Encourage people to build permanent fixtures on others' land.

    D. Indicate the case is meaningless.

C. Watch the video and fill in the blanks.

A common law system is essentially a legal system that follows the rules set in (1) _____ . This is the (2) _____ of the United States, England and many other territories. But this is not to say that our common law (3) _____ as it did in Blackstone's time. Our law is (4) _____ . The American common law system began with the (5) _____ of Blackstone's English common law, but today, it includes centuries of subsequent American law.

D. Watch the video and decide whether the following statements are true or false.

[ ] 1. Only the English common law remains an important part of our current U.S. law system.

[ ] 2. Blackstone's *Commentaries* created the United States Supreme Court through Article III.

[ ] 3. The Supreme Court's rulings are the last and final word.

[ ] 4. Early Supreme Court decisions cited the *Commentaries* rarely.

[ ] 5. New case law decisions then become a part of American common law system.

E. Watch the video and fill in the blanks.

Let's review. The English common law system was developed over centuries and is based on the (1) _____ of right and wrong originally established by ancient tribal peoples. Decision-makers issued decisions based on these customs, and future disputes were bound by these decisions. Our early colonists adopted this common law system, which was (2) _____. Around the time of the American Revolution, Sir William Blackstone published his *Commentaries* as a (3) _____ of the English common law. This publication continues to (4) _____. Our framers established our Supreme Court and our Congress. Together, these two (5) _____ make and (6) _____. These newer laws build on Blackstone's work and American case law to form what we know as our modern American common law system.

Part IV Speaking Task

This video mentioned a movement of court hearing. Let's appreciate this scene of the TV series "Justice," then use your own words to retell the story as much as you can based on the following instruction.

1. What was Luther Graves's career before he became a lawyer?

_____

_____

2. As Luther Graves said, why do we have juries?

_____

_____

Lesson 2
FUNDAMENTAL DOCTRINE: STARE DECISIS DOCTRINE

Part I　Getting Ready

The following words and phrases will appear in this unit. Use five minutes to find out the meanings of these words and phrases.

Listen carefully and study them.

1. Stare decisis
2. Precedent
3. Appellate
4. Issue a court ruling
5. Infringe
6. Defendant
7. Witness
8. Advocate
9. Prosecutor
10. Jurisdiction

Part II Overview

Definition and Demonstrations of Stare Decisis

A. Complete the paragraphs below with one word in each gap.

Stare decisis is a Latin term. It means "to stand by things decided." Stare decisis is a doctrine used in all court cases and with all legal issues. A doctrine is simply a (1)_____, or an instruction, but it's not necessarily a rule that cannot ever be (2)_____.

The doctrine of stare decisis means that (3)_____ look to past, similar issues to (4)_____ their decisions. The past decisions are known as precedent. Precedent is a legal principle or rule that is created by a court (5)_____. This decision becomes an example, or (6)_____, for judges deciding similar issues later. Stare decisis is the doctrine that (7)_____ courts to look to precedent when making their decisions. These two principles allow American law to build (8)_____, and make the legal system a common law system.

B. Listen and comprehend. Fill in the blanks with words or phrases mentioned in the listening material.

In the example, Blue borrows Red's lawnmower, so Blue is a (1)_____ and Red is a (2)_____. Red discovers that Blue uses the lawnmower without his (3)_____, and (4)_____ the lawnmower. Red sues and (5)_____ Blue buy him a new one, but the court only decides that Blue does (6)_____ Red the money required to (7)_____ it. The decision turns to precedent, and lower court in the same (8)_____ should have to follow it.

Lesson 2
Fundamental Doctrine: Stare Decisis Doctrine

C. Decide whether the statements below are true or false.

[ ] 1. Courts are expected to follow their own previous rulings only.

[ ] 2. Lower courts are expected to follow the rule made by higher courts. For example, the Texas state appellate courts should follow rulings of the South Carolina Supreme Court.

[ ] 3. The U.S. Supreme Court issues a court ruling that taxes are unconstitutional. This decision is binding all courts in the U.S.

[ ] 4. There is a possibility for South Carolina to follow Texas rule.

D. Answer the questions.

1. What is the Roe v. Wade case about?

   _____
   _____

2. Why did the Supreme Court decline to follow precedent set in the Roe v. Wade case?

   _____
   _____

3. What happened in the 1950s and 1960s?

   _____
   _____

4. When can the precedent be abandoned?

   _____
   _____

Part III Further Understanding

A. Decide whether the statements below are true or false.

[ ] 1. The high court changed the policy known as affirmative action in its decision.

[ ] 2. Fisher's lawyers argued that race shouldn't be considered in the admission process, or constitutional rights would be infringed.

[ ] 3. The majority of justices thought the Supreme Court had not fully studied the university's actions.

[ ] 4. Both opponents and civil rights activists were satisfied with the decision of the Supreme Court.

B. Complete the paragraphs below with words or phrases.

On Wednesday morning, a different crowd waited outside the court building. Supporters of (1)_____ cheered when the Supreme Court canceled (2)_____ on the issue.

The court said the 1996 federal law called the (3)_____ of Marriage Act (4)_____ the rights of same-sex couples. The court said that the government could not prevent same-sex couples from getting (5)_____ as traditional husbands and wives. Supporters of the laws promised to (6)_____ marriage to legal unions of one man and one woman.

Lesson 2
Fundamental Doctrine: Stare Decisis Doctrine

Part IV Speaking Task

A. This conversation mentioned a movement of court hearing. Let's appreciate this scene of the movie "To Kill a Mocking Bird" about Mr. Atticus.
Now you are supposed to answer the following questions orally. Please try to be as brief as you can; practice with your partner.

1. Did the defendant agree with the testimony of two witnesses?

2. What kind of disability does the defendant have?

3. Please use two words to describe Mayella Ewell.

4. What rigid code of society did Mayella break?

5. Was the defendant guilty or not guilty actually?

B. This conversation mentioned a movement of court hearing. Let's appreciate this scene of the movie "A Devil's Advocate" about Mr. Lomax and Mr. Alexander Cullen. Choose the best answer for each question.

1. Why was Mr. Cullen accused?

    A. He cheated others.

    B. He killed three people on purpose.

    C. He killed his wives and his stepchildren.

2. Who is Mr. Brogo?

    A. The judge.

    B. The prosecutor.

    C. The witness.

3. Why did Mr. Lomax try to make the jury hate Mr. Cullen?

    A. He disliked Mr. Cullen.

    B. He knew Mr. Cullen was guilty and he didn't want to advocate for him.

    C. He tried to prove an alibi.

4. Which description is most suitable for Mr. Cullen?

    A. He is a bad husband but a good father.

    B. He has a successful career.

    C. It's his first time to break law.

Lesson 3
SOURCES OF LAW (1)

Part I   Getting Ready

The following words and phrases will appear in this unit. Use five minutes to find out the meanings of these words and phrases.

Listen carefully and study them.

1. Executive
2. Legislative
3. The Bill of Rights
4. Congress
5. Amendment
6. Nominate
7. Judicial review
8. Vague
9. Delegate
10. Budget

Part II Overview

A. (a) Watch the video and choose the best answer for each question.

1. What is the main purpose of the executive branch?

    A. To oversee the federal government.

    B. To uphold the Constitution.

    C. To carry out laws.

    D. To appoint members to the other branches.

2. What is the main purpose of the legislative branch?

    A. To make laws.

    B. To uphold the Constitution.

    C. To carry out laws.

    D. To oversee the federal government.

3. What is the main purpose of the judicial branch?

    A. To make laws.

    B. To uphold the Constitution.

    C. To carry out laws.

    D. To appoint members to the other branches.

(b) Match these three parts of government with the three branches.

The Congress	legislative branch
The president	judicial branch
The Supreme Court	executive branch

Lesson 3
Sources of Law (1)

B. Watch the video and fill in the blanks.

When we talk about constitutional law, we are talking about many different types of laws that cover many different (1)_____. Much of constitutional law has to do with the (2)_____ of the Constitution. Specifically, constitutional law deals with the basic relationships between the different (3)_____ in our society. These relationships include those between the states, the states and the federal government, the three (4)_____ of the federal government, the federal government and foreign (5)_____, individuals and state government, and individuals and the federal government.

C. Watch the video and decide whether the following statements are true or false.

[ ] 1. The Constitution would never have been signed without The Bill of Rights.

[ ] 2. There were originally twelve amendments, but it was the right-assuring list of ten that made it into the Constitution.

[ ] 3. The Bill of Rights did get the Constitution ratified, but the rights of U.S. citizens are not protected as much as other developed countries.

D. Watch the video and answer the following questions.

1. What are the components of the U.S. Congress?

   _____
   _____

2. What does Article II of the U.S. Constitution establish?

   _____
   _____

3. Which article of the Constitution is known as the supremacy clause?

   _____
   _____

4. What is the most famous amendment of the U.S. Constitution?

   _____

   _____

5. Which article states that the Constitution is the highest law of the land?

   _____

   _____

Part III Further Understanding

A. Watch the video and fill in the blanks.

1. Generally speaking, _____ makes our laws.
2. Together, the two _____ of Congress have various important powers.
3. Our Congress is made up of _____ from each state.
4. A state's _____ determines the number of representatives per state.
5. The U.S. vice president serves as the head of the _____ but doesn't vote unless there is a tie.

B. Watch the video and fill in the blanks.

Article II of the United States Constitution created and empowered our executive branch of government. The United States (1) _____ leads the executive branch, which also includes the president's (2) _____, the 15-member cabinet and all federal agencies. Our president serves as our chief (3) _____, or commander-in-chief. This branch is responsible for (4) _____ out laws. Among other significant duties, the executive branch enforces and recommends federal laws, proposes a federal (5) _____, directs our foreign policy, commands the Armed Forces and nominates and appoints federal government officials. The president may veto or approve

Lesson 3
Sources of Law (1)

legislation, which serves as a check on Congress' authority. The president may also grant (6)_____ and amnesty, which serves as a check on the judicial branch. The president is elected through a (7)_____ public election. Presidential elections are held every four years. The president may serve up to two (8)_____ of four years each.

C. Watch the video and decide whether the following statements are true or false.

[ ] 1. The judicial branch only includes the United States Supreme Court all lower federal courts.

[ ] 2. Judicial powers include deciding cases on appeal from lower federal or state courts and deciding cases involving a state-vs.-state issue or a branch-vs.-branch issue.

[ ] 3. The Supreme Court's power of judicial review comes directly from the Constitution.

[ ] 4. Through judicial review, the Supreme Court reviews federal legislation to determine if the laws passed by Congress are in keeping with the Constitution.

[ ] 5. The Supreme Court includes 9 justices, 9 associate justices and 1 chief justice.

Part IV Speaking Task

This conversation mentioned a movement of court hearing. Let's appreciate this scene of the TV series "The Good Wife" about Mrs. Florrick's confrontation with Mr. Polmar, then discuss the questions with your partner.

1. Which two implications may "vague" include according to the text?

_____

_____

2. When Mr. Polmar indicated that Mr. Roja, at one time, worked for Mr. Bishop "in his... drug empire," how did Mrs. Florrick object?

_____
_____

Lesson 4

SOURCES OF LAW (2)

Part I Getting Ready

The following words and phrases will appear in this unit. Use five minutes to find out the meanings of these words and phrases.

Listen carefully and study them.

1. Supremacy Clause
2. Prohibit
3. Confederation
4. Elastic clause
5. Foregoing powers
6. Administrative law
7. Privilege
8. Immunity
9. Ordinance
10. Proceeding

Part II Overview

Constitution and Federalism

A. Watch the video and decide whether the following statements are true or false.

[ ] 1. The Supremacy Clause states that the "Constitution, and the Laws of the United States which shall be made in Pursuance thereof…shall be the Supreme Law of the Land."

[ ] 2. The Supremacy Clause just prohibits state governments from passing laws that conflict with federal laws, but it does not prohibit other entity from enforcing laws that are in conflict with the Constitution.

[ ] 3. Under the Articles of Confederation, the federal government was absolutely weak.

[ ] 4. The state of Kentucky is allowed to save millions of dollars by requiring citizens to pay for their own criminal trials.

B. Watch the video and fill in the blanks.

The necessary and proper clause is one of the most (1)_____ clauses in the Constitution. Generally speaking, this clause allows Congress to make any law it deems essential and appropriate. This clause is often called the "elastic clause" because it (2)_____ the powers of Congress beyond the powers already enumerated in the Constitution. Enumerated powers are those that are specifically set out in the (3)_____ and are defined in the clause as "foregoing powers." The (4)_____ clause can be stretched to include many different types of laws covering many different issues. This clause states that Congress can "make all laws which shall be necessary and proper for carrying into (5)_____ the foregoing powers, and all other powers vested by this Constitution." It works as a "catch-all." There are

Lesson 4
Sources of Law (2)

many powers already given to Congress in Article I. The necessary and proper clause tells Congress that it can (6)_____ make any law it believes it needs to make in order to carry out those powers. For example, through the necessary and proper clause, Congress established the federal judicial system and enacted a large body of federal (7)_____, though neither one of these duties is (8)_____ through the Constitution.

C. Watch the video and choose the best answer for each question.

1. In the United States, citizens are subject to federal, state, and local laws. This is known as _____.

    A. unitary government

    B. confederacy

    C. federation

    D. federalism

2. In some countries, one unit holds the power. This is known as _____.

    A. unitary government

    B. confederacy

    C. federation

    D. federalism

3. Which is an association of independent governmental units?

    A. Unitary government.

    B. Confederacy.

    C. Federation.

    D. Federalism.

D. Watch the video and answer the following questions.

1. What is administrative law sometimes called?

2. What does administrative law cover?

3. What are the two types of administrative law?

4. Who has the power to enact administrative law?

5. Who usually specifies how administrative law should be used?

E. (a) Watch the video and decide whether the following statements are true or false.

[ ] 1. The privileges and immunities clauses can be found in Article V of the United States Constitution and in the Fourteenth Amendment to the Constitution.

[ ] 2. The framers added the first privileges and immunities clause in hopes of guaranteeing the same general rights everywhere in the U.S. and of encouraging travel between the states.

[ ] 3. The first privileges and immunities clause was added after the abolition of slavery and as a part of the Fourteenth Amendment's equal protection guarantees.

[ ] 4. These two clauses work together to restrict the fundamental constitutional rights of individual United States citizens.

Lesson 4
Sources of Law (2)

(b) Listen to the text and answer the following questions.

1. What benefit can out-of-state citizens get from the privileges and immunities clauses?

   _____

   _____

2. What activity is exempt from the privileges and immunities clauses?

   _____

   _____

F. Watch the video and choose the best answer for each question.

1. The United States' original full faith and credit clause appeared in _____.

   A. the Declaration of Independence

   B. the Treaty of Paris

   C. the U.S. Constitution

   D. the Bill of Rights

   E. the Articles of Confederation

2. The main purpose of the full faith and credit clause is to _____.

   A. ensure that states honor the court judgments of other states

   B. ensure that states grant credit to the citizens of other states

   C. ensure that U.S. citizens can sue in any court, in any state, that they wish

   D. ensure that plaintiffs receive the largest money judgment possible

   E. ensure that bankruptcy cases are only tried in the federal courts

Part III Speaking Task

Let's appreciate a short episode from the American TV series "Person of Interest." In this episode, with the intention of preventing the crime before it happened, Mr. Finch desired to take Mr. Reese into partnership.

A. Listen to the text and decide whether the following statements are true or false.

    [ ] 1. Mr. Reese used to work for the government.

    [ ] 2. Mr. Reese has spent the last couple of months trying to drink himself to death.

    [ ] 3. The government knows that Mr. Reese is alive.

    [ ] 4. According to this text, someone is murdered in New York City every 80 hours.

B. Retell the story in your own words.

Lesson 5

COMPARISON OF LAWS

Part I   Getting Ready

The following words and phrases will appear in this unit. Use five minutes to find out the meanings of these words and phrases.

Listen carefully and study them.

1. Acquitted
2. Liable
3. Legal dispute
4. Cause of action
5. Prosecution
6. Parties
7. Plaintiff
8. Burden of proof
9. Beyond a reasonable doubt
10. Preponderance of the evidence
11. Legal remedy
12. Be convicted

Part II Overview

Public Law vs. Private Law

A. Watch the video and match the categories of law with the simple definition.

1. Public law

   Criminal laws (   )

   International laws (   )

   Administrative laws (   )

   Constitutional laws (   )

   Municipal laws (   )

   a. that govern government agencies, like the Department of Education and the Equal Employment Opportunity Commission

   b. that relate to crime

   c. that are ordinances, regulations and by-laws that govern a city or town

   d. that protect citizens' rights as afforded in the Constitution

   e. that oversee relations between nations

2. Private law

   Tort law (   )

   Succession law (   )

   Contract law (   )

   Family law (   )

   Property law (   )

Lesson 5
Comparison of Laws

a. governs forms of property ownership, transfer and tenant issues

b. governs the transfer of an estate between parties

c. governs rights and obligations of those entering into contracts

d. covers rights, obligations and remedies provided to someone who has been wronged by another individual

e. governs family-related and domestic-related issues

B. Listen to the material and fill in the blanks.

The main difference between public and private law is in the parties that each affects.

Public law affects society as a whole and includes (1) _____ law, constitutional law, criminal law, municipal law and international law. In the landmark case of Brown v. Board of Education, it clearly (2) _____ the way public law works. In Brown v. Board of Education, a small child's rights were (3) _____ by an administrative agency. The family brought suit upon the agency and won.

Private law, on the other hand, affects individuals, families, businesses and small groups. Its scope is not as wide as public law and includes contract law, tort law, property law, (4) _____ law and family law. In Carvajal v. Hillstone Restaurant Group, Inc. we learned that the (5) _____ Carvajal, was harmed as a result of eating a whole artichoke. He claims the server did not inform or instruct him on the proper way to consume the vegetable. Carvajal became ill as a result and sought (6) _____ for his pain and (7) _____ as a matter of tort law.

Part III Further Understanding

Criminal Law vs. Civil Law

A. Watch the video and write the missing sentences.

(1) _____ Criminal law involves the government's prosecution of a defendant, who is accused of a crime.

(2) _____, meaning a real doubt, based upon reason and common sense, after careful and impartial consideration of all the evidence.

(3) _____ Civil law involves a plaintiff's lawsuit against a defendant.

(4) _____ The plaintiff must prove his or her lawsuit by a preponderance of the evidence, which means more than 50% of the evidence supports that party's legal assertion. (5) _____

_____

B. Watch the video and decide whether the following statements are true or false.

[   ] 1. Prosecution can be used in civil law.

[   ] 2. The person charged with the crime is known as the defendant, but the party initiating a civil case is known as the plaintiff.

[   ] 3. A burden of proof is the obligation to substantiate the case.

[   ] 4. The burden of proof for the plaintiff in criminal law is much lower than that for prosecutions in civil law.

[   ] 5. The defendant in a civil case will not be convicted or punished.

Lesson 5
Comparison of Laws

C. Watch the video and put the sentences A-E in the right places.

(1) _____ These rules, or laws, define crimes and set forth punishment. They also define our rights and responsibilities as citizens. There are elements of substantive law in both criminal and civil law.

Civil law differs from criminal law in that it applies to interactions between citizens. (2) _____ For example, if you sue a neighbor for cutting down a tree and letting it land on your house, that would be a civil case dealing with tort rather than a criminal case dealing with crime.

(3) _____ Let's say a person is caught drunk driving. Substantive law says that it is a crime punishable by a term in prison.

(4) _____ In other words, specific facts need to be proven true in order to convict somebody of a crime or a tort.

In the case of a person caught driving while intoxicated, a few things would have to be proven:

- The person was driving the vehicle.
- (5) _____
- The person was over the legal limit per a field sobriety and/or Breathalyzer test.

Once these things are proven, the person can be taken into custody. Next, procedural law will determine the steps the case must take.

A. Substantive law is used to determine whether a crime or tort has been committed, define what charges may apply and decide whether the evidence supports the charges.

B. Rather than dealing with crime, civil law deals with tort, or actions that aren't necessarily illegal but can be proven to be damaging in some way.

C. The substance of charges, or elements of a crime or tort, must be carefully evaluated to determine whether a crime or tort really exists.

D. The person acted in ways that gave the police a reason to believe he or she was intoxicated.

E. Substantive law consists of written statutory rules passed by legislature that govern how people behave.

D. Watch the video and answer the following questions.

1. What is the right about procedural law granted by the 14th Amendment to U.S. citizens?

2. What does due process mean and what benefits does it bring to the citizens?

3. According to the 14th Amendment, if someone is arrested, what rights does he have?

E. Watch the video and choose the right answer.

1. What happened to the victim according to the sheriff?

    A. She was raped.

    B. She was beaten up.

    C. She was raped and beaten up.

2. Who has the burden of proof?

    A. The victim.

    B. The prosecutor.

    C. The court.

Lesson 5
Comparison of Laws

3. Who are the parties of this case?

    A. The victim and the prosecutor.

    B. The victim and the defendant.

    C. The prosecutor and the defendant.

Part IV Speaking Task

Share your understanding with the class of which law in the case is concerned and why.

Lesson 6

TYPES OF LEGAL ACTIONS

Part I Getting Ready

The following words and phrases will appear in this unit. Use five minutes to find out the meanings of these words and phrases.

Listen carefully and study them.

1. Disagreement
2. Subject matter
3. Arrest
4. Trial
5. Settle
6. Interpretation of the law
7. Prosecution
8. The U.S. Circuit Court of Appeals
9. The U.S. District Court
10. Preside

Lesson 6
Types of Legal Actions

Part II Overview

Criminal Action and Civil Action

A. Watch the video and fill in the blanks.

When something happens, whether it is a criminal action or a civil disagreement between neighbors, the case is taken to the trial court. The (1)_____ is the initial court a case moves through based on jurisdiction. You've likely heard the term jurisdiction before. In the court system, (2)_____ is the power that a court holds to oversee a trial or other legal orders. It can be based on several things:

- Jurisdiction over the person involved in the civil or criminal activity;
- Jurisdiction over the (3)_____ ;
- Jurisdiction to render a particular (4)_____ sought (limits over court power; e.g., small (5)_____ court can hear cases under a certain dollar value)

B. Watch the video and put the following sentences in the correct order.

1. (   )

   (1) The arrested party makes an initial appearance where the party learns the charges.

   (2) If either party is not satisfied, an appeal can be filed with a higher court to review the existing evidence.

   (3) An arrest is made.

   (4) An arraignment is held where the arrested person enters a plea of guilty or not guilty.

   (5) A preliminary hearing is set, and the judge will listen to any testimony from witnesses to determine whether there is actually a case.

(6) The arrested person stands trial before a judge and jury where both the plaintiff and the defendant present evidence and a judgment is made.

2. (   )

(1) The judge or jury makes a decision based on the facts of the case.

(2) The plaintiff initiates a complaint with the court for the wrongdoing.

(3) Plaintiff and defendant (generally through their attorneys) exchange facts about the case. This is called discovery.

(4) Either party may file an appeal.

(5) Complaint is delivered to the defendant; the defendant has a certain period of time to respond or the case is forfeited to the benefit of the plaintiff.

(6) A trial is presented to a judge.

C. Watch the video and decide whether the following statements are true or false.

The evidence will be presented in different ways between trail court and appellate court.

[ ] 1. The appellate court reviews evidence and outcomes of cases that have been settled in any court when one party was not satisfied with the decision.

[ ] 2. The trial in the appellate court is about the review of evidence and outcome.

[ ] 3. The Supreme Court only deals with matters of state or national importance or appeals from appellate court.

[ ] 4. The Supreme Court will take cases from appellate court only if there was an issue with the interpretation of constitutional rights. It is the last step in the appeals process.

Lesson 6
Types of Legal Actions

Part III Further Understanding

Types of Courts

A. Watch the video and answer the following questions.

(a)

1. When can a civil action be heard in the U.S. District Court?

_____
_____

2. Who has the right to determine findings of facts?

_____
_____

(b)

1. How many U.S. Circuit Court of Appeals are there in the United States?

_____
_____

2. Why are there only three judges who hear a case when there are 179 full-time circuit judges?

_____
_____

B. Watch the video and write down the missing sentences.

There are three main levels of federal court system. (1) _____ The U.S. District Court has jurisdiction over cases involving both civil and criminal actions. (2) _____, a violation of law or treaties of the United States or if the United States is party to the suit. (3) _____

35

(4)_____ The cases are brought up from the lower U.S. District Court. (5)_____

C. Watch the video and put the sentences in the right places.

The U.S. Supreme Court is the highest court in the United States and resides over cases of national importance. (1)_____ Each justice is nominated by the President of the United States and appointed by Senate. The justices are given a lifetime term and can end only by resignation, retirement or impeachment. (2)_____

Subject-matter cases generally involve disputes between two states, diversity cases where each party resides in different states and the dispute exceeds $75,000, disputes with foreign nationals, treaty issues or cases where the United States is party to the case. Appeals are heard only when there has been a violation of Constitutional law in the decision of a lower court. (3)_____ In a death penalty case, the vote must render a 5 of 9 ratios. If granted, the case will be reviewed based on the facts and the decision. (4)_____ If the case is denied, there is no further action. The case is considered closed. This does not imply agreement with the lower court decision by this court. (5)_____

A. In order to have a case heard, a writ of certiorari must be granted in a 4 of 9 votes by the justices.

B. It is presided over by nine justices, including one chief justice and eight associate justices.

C. Chances are, the writ will be denied as these judges hear only a small percentage of cases —150 of the thousands requested per year.

D. It simply means there was not enough evidence to convince the panel of justices that a wrongdoing occurred.

E. There are two types of cases heard by the justices: subject-matter cases and appeals from lower courts.

Lesson 6
Types of Legal Actions

D. Watch the video and choose the right answer to each question.

1. Who is the Plaintiff?

    A. Mr. Putnam.

    B. Miss Putnam.

    C. Miss Paula.

2. What happened to the plaintiff?

    A. The plaintiff was injured in a car accident.

    B. The plaintiff was dismissed from her job.

    C. The plaintiff suffered a sexual offend.

3. How does the lawyer call the judge?

    A. My lord.

    B. My honor.

    C. Your honor.

Part IV Speaking Task

Watch the video and discuss the answers to the following questions with your partner.

1. Can the justices in the U.S. Supreme Court be the justices for their whole life?

   _____
   _____

2. What should the losing party do if they want their case to be reviewed by the U.S. Supreme Court?

   _____
   _____

3. How can the parties get a final decision?

Part V   Case Study

A. Watch the video and answer the following questions.

1. Why does this trail try in the U.S. District Court?

2. What is the final decision?

B. Watch the video and answer the following questions.

1. What is the decision of the trial court?

2. What does the appellate court do and what is the final decision?

C. Watch the video and answer the following questions.

1. What law does this case involve?

Lesson 6
Types of Legal Actions

2. Does this law belong to private law or public law?

   _____

   _____

3. What is the final decision of this case?

   _____

   _____

4. What are the grounds for the decision?

   _____

   _____

Lesson 7
LEGAL PROCEDURES

Part I   Getting Ready

The following words and phrases will appear in this unit. Use five minutes to find out the meanings of these words and phrases.

Listen carefully and study them.

1. Plaintiff
2. Defendant
3. Complaint
4. Counterclaim
5. Discovery
6. Testimony
7. Deposition
8. Accuse
9. Reverse the jury's decision
10. Certiorari

Lesson 7
Legal Procedures

Part II Overview

Courts

A. Listen to the text and try to give definition of the terms below according to what you have heard.

Plaintiff _____

Defendant _____

Lawyer _____

Judge _____

B. Here are several sentences about initiation of a lawsuit. Listen to the text and arrange them in the right order.

    A. The plaintiff files a complaint with the court and a summons is delivered to the defendant.

    B. A judge or jury hears the case and a judgment is made.

    C. If either party is not satisfied with the outcome, an appeal may be filed with a higher court.

    D. The defendant answers the complaint and may counterclaim against the plaintiff.

    E. Discovery of testimony through interrogatories and depositions take place.

C. Listen to the text and fill in the blanks with the word or words you have heard.

    Once a person believes they have been wronged and wants to sue, the first thing done is the filing of a (1)_____, a written statement containing claims of damages one suffered as a result of another person. This is the plaintiff.

Each wrongful act is considered a separate (2)_____ in the complaint. And there can be several causes of action in only one complaint. These are the legal grounds and the facts of the case. The complaint serves to let the defendant know that impending legal action is coming his way.

Once a complaint has been filed, the defendant is notified by way of a (3)_____, or an official notice from the court that an action is being taken against the defendant. It also states where the defendant must appear.

The defendant has 20-30 days to file an (4)_____ with the court. The answer contains the defendant's response to the claim against him. If the defendant neglects to answer to the claims against him, a (5)_____ will be granted in favor of the plaintiff. In other words, the plaintiff wins by default. Sometimes, the defendant may decide to file a (6)_____ against the plaintiff. This is similar to the original complaint, but accuses the plaintiff of an action.

To set this into (7)_____, Jim was driving east on a dark road. He neglected to turn his headlights on. Dennis was driving west on the same dark road. Dennis crashed into Jim causing major damage to Jim's car.

Jim (8)_____ against Dennis for negligence. Fair enough, Dennis should have been more careful when driving on a dark road. However, Dennis was not completely convinced that he was 100% at fault. After all, Jim was driving without headlights.

Dennis can file a counterclaim stating that the accident was not totally his fault. Having headlights been on, he would have seen Jim barreling down the road and avoided careening into his car.

(9)_____ about the case must be presented. This information is mined through (10)_____, and is the opportunity to gain information and evidence from the other party. This is done in a couple of ways.

(11)_____ and depositions provide information based on testimony. There is a difference between interrogatories and depositions. Interrogatories are written

Lesson 7
Legal Procedures

answers to specific questions posed by the other party. (12)_____ are oral arguments in response to questions asked by the other party. Once all of the evidence and testimony is gathered, the case goes before a judge.

Part III Speaking Task

A. Listen to the text and discuss the answers to the questions below.

You can take notes while you are listening.

1. What is a complaint?

   _____

2. What elements does a complaint include?

   _____

3. What will be included in a summons?

   _____

B. Listen to the text and discuss the answers to the questions below.

You can take notes while you are listening.

1. What is the result if the defendant refuses to answer to the summons?

   _____

2. What does information negotiation refer to?

   _____

3. What if Mills and Gritty cannot reach an agreement?

   _____

Part IV Further Understanding

Jury

A. Listen to the text and decide whether the following statements are true or false.

[ ] 1. The most common type of verdicts is the special verdict.

[ ] 2. Another verdict type is the special verdict and is saved for less complex questions of fact.

[ ] 3. Having listened to the plaintiff, deciding that no legal case exists and rules in favor of the defendant, a judge will give a directed verdict.

[ ] 4. The burden of proof is not always placed on the plaintiff.

B. Listen to the text and decide whether the following statements are true or false.

[ ] 1. When there is a hung jury, a mistrial is declared and a new trial must begin.

[ ] 2. If a jury's decision is approved, a judgment notwithstanding the verdict will be made by the judge.

[ ] 3. In a motion to dismiss, the defendant may ask the court to dismiss the case totally.

[ ] 4. The judge can never reverse the jury's decision.

C. Listen to the text and write a summary about civil appeals process (no more than 200 words).

_____

_____

_____

_____

Lesson 8

AMERICAN CONSTITUTION — STATE AND FEDERAL CONFLICT

Part I Getting Ready

The following words and phrases will appear in this unit. Use five minutes to find out the meanings of these words and phrases.

Listen carefully and study them.

1. Delineate
2. Entrench
3. Bicameral
4. Doctrine
5. Momentous
6. NATO
7. Levy
8. Deploy
9. Cannabis
10. Marijuana
11. Apothecary
12. Sulfur dioxide

Part II Overview

Basic Introduction of American Constitutions

A. Fill in the blanks, and decide whether the following statements are true or false.

Travel around America, and you are (1) _____ to run into the constitution. It seems to be everywhere. This little document, it means everything to us. We (2) _____ the constitution and for good reasons. It was (3) _____. An owner's (4) _____ for a new nation, setting up an entirely new form of government. It's like the big bang. It's the (5) _____ to happen in the modern world. But more than two centuries later, many of us do not have any idea what the constitution says. Of course, that has never stopped us from arguing what it means.

[ ] 1. It is a turning point in American history, to have the new constitution.

[ ] 2. The states were closely connected when the constitution came along.

[ ] 3. The first frame work of the constitution was drafted in 1787.

[ ] 4. The states find it easy to reach an agreement under the constitution.

[ ] 5. The states can exert influences on the decision of the federal government.

B. Fill in the blanks.

Before the constitution comes along, each state is basically almost its own nation, the thirteen states are connected together by a (1) _____ kind of like NATO, or the EU. Akyl is talking about the articles of federation. That was the first (2) _____ for American government. It was drafted back in 1777, during the American Revolution. It was so loose that they actually called it a "league of friendship." As if the states (3) _____, they were just friends. The confederation congress could not (4) _____, and even raising an

Lesson 8
American Constitution—State and Federal Conflict

army was a challenge. It has to beg the states for contributions. In fact, it could not do much of anything, unless at least two thirds of the states were in agreement. With this crowd, agreement was not a (5) _____. The states have been colonies for decades, and for some cases, centuries before the American Revolution, they were separate ones from each other. If someone actually (6) _____, with an army of the world, president of the world, and a legislature of the world. There is one thing that could make you go for that today, if the (7) _____.

How Did American Constitution Come into Being?

A. Decide whether the following statements are true or false.

[ ] 1. Lack of power to tax and deepening debts make the government difficult to run.

[ ] 2. It took the delegates five months to come up with a compromise of the new form of government.

[ ] 3. Before the new confederation, small states do not have much to say compared with larger states.

[ ] 4. There is no big differences of government the new constitution created, apart from no chief of executive.

[ ] 5. The new government still cannot levy taxes or raise an army.

B. Fill in the blanks.

Who called the commission, who decided it? Well, a group of (1) _____, most (2) _____ Alexander Hamilton and James Madison. They had seen that the ways in which the government under the articles had put this (3) _____ in danger. The lack of power to tax, deepening debts, 9 states had their own navies, Shays' rebellion in Massachusetts, so there's civil unrest. So they really did have a sense of crisis, they got to do something, to (4) _____.

This is James Madison's great (5) _____. He came to the convention with his own plan, that he worked on the Spring of 1787. That plan called scraping the articles all together and created a nation, in their words, "a (6) _____" with the supreme legislature, executive and (7) _____. That set the tone for the debate from that time on.

C. Watch again, and answer the questions.

1. What did the men do before coming up with a plan for how the states could be represented?
   _____
   _____

2. How many senates are there in one state?
   _____
   _____

3. What do you think were the most distinguished new features in the new Constitution?
   _____
   _____

State and Federal Conflicts

A. Decide whether the following statements are true or false.

[ ] 1. From the listening, we know that California has been a place of constitutional battle ground.

[ ] 2. The founders created this state and federal system 215 years ago.

B. Fill in the missing information based on what you have heard.

The problem is, this is Cannabis, (1) _____. Here we are in Northern California, in the Emerald Triangle. This is perfectly legal here. The owners have been

Lesson 8
American Constitution—State and Federal Conflict

(2) _____ about following California state law. However, under federal law, this is a terrible crime. At any minute, (3) _____ could appear here and arrest everybody, seize all these, and send them all to prison.

Marijuana in Harbor Site

A. Listen to the passage and decide whether the following statements are true or false.

[ ] 1. Harbor site has its own apothecary system, created by a scientist.

[ ] 2. Medical marijuana can be used to treat different kinds of diseases.

[ ] 3. You can receive a death penalty if you distribute 600000 Cannabis plants.

B. Answer these questions.

1. Why is Stephen considered to be a good Californian?

   _____

   _____

2. What kinds of acute and chronic diseases can medical marijuana serve?

   _____

   _____

Part III Further Understanding

Federal Government's Merits—Depression

Listen and answer the following questions.

1. In the early 1930s, what has happened?

   _____

   _____

2. What contribution has president Roosevelt made to America?

　_____

　_____

3. FDR changed that. He pumped money into the economy to try to _____ _____. He started massive federal building project to put people back to work. As Roosevelt nursed the economy back to health, he created an alphabet suit of federal agencies. They are now an economic safety net, an old age _____, called social security. Of course, it did not happen without _____.

Part IV　Case Study

A. Decide whether the following statements are true or false.

[ ] 1. No one believes it so strongly that the federal government can be trusted to make correct choices.

[ ] 2. Golden gate bridge is the collaboration work of federal government and state government.

[ ] 3. To solve cross state issues, federal government should come into play.

[ ] 4. The system, produced on a chain of law, is better than those on arms.

B. Fill in the blanks.

　　No one again has the (1) _____ to do that, sometimes they lack the information to do it, that's sort of (2) _____ for the federal roles and those kinds of standards. But there isn't a competing interest of liberty, let's say the state like Kentucky has a lot of coals, and it makes a lot of (3) _____ for them to burn their coals. That's the argument you hear a lot, that the states should get to choose

Lesson 8
American Constitution—State and Federal Conflict

what level of protection, but the problem is that when you burn the coals and you produce (4) _____, soot, and smog, that drift from Kentucky to other states, you create a (5) _____ problem.

It seems we have been having the same debate for (6) _____. Trying to figure out who should win the (7) _____ between the states and the federal government. The issues may have changed, but the struggle for power just goes on and on.

Lesson 9
LEGAL CONCEPTS (1): BILL OF RIGHTS (US)

Part I Getting Ready

The following words and phrases will appear in this unit. Use five minutes to find out the meanings of these words and phrases.

Listen carefully and study them.

1. Confer
2. Enact
3. Ratified
4. Periphery
5. Flog
6. Deformation
7. Penitentiary
8. Sentence convict
9. Interrogation
10. Eminent domain
11. Warp drive speed

Lesson 9
Legal Concepts (1): Bill of Rights (US)

Part II Overview

Listen to the text and answer the following questions.

1. What is the constitutional idea according to the first speaker?

   _____

   _____

2. What is the function of "the Bill of Rights" according to the text?

   _____

   _____

The Ten Amendments

Listen and write down the content for each amendment.

The first amendment includes _____

The second amendment includes _____

The third amendment is _____

The fourth amendment secures _____

The fifth amendment protects _____

The six amendment ensures _____

The seventh amendment guarantees _____

The eighth amendment protects _____

The ninth amendment declares _____

The tenth amendment says _____

Akhil Amar from Yale University

Fill in the blanks.

It doesn't just come from a closed meeting at Philadelphia. It comes from 13 very (1) _____, and opens to the world over a whole year. People were talking about the thing, so it comes from the (2) _____. It's written in a way that is very easy to understand, very easy to memorize, so becomes part of the culture. It's this (3) _____.

The language of the Bill of Rights seems very (4) _____, but that hasn't stopped us from arguing about it. Some of the arguments have been bitter, and the issues painful. But those arguments have sometimes led to the most important (5) _____.

Part III Further Understanding

Albert Snider, a Father

Decide whether the following statements are true or false.

[ ] 1. Westboro Baptist is a religious group that fights against homosexuality.

[ ] 2. It is against the God's will for being gay, according to this religious group.

[ ] 3. Snider's father sued the group for deformation of his son's character.

[ ] 4. According to Snider's father, the freedom speech should not deprive other's rights.

Lesson 9
Legal Concepts (1): Bill of Rights (US)

What's Going on with Freedom to Speak

Fill in the blanks.

In our country there has always been (1) _____, between an abstract right to free speech and how much we hate when somebody is actually saying. Our country's (2) _____ has been tested over and over. During World War I, Americans were swept up in a patriotic fervor, and congress made it a crime to interfere with the war effort. And banned (3) _____ about the government, the flag or the army forces. When communists spoke their political views out aloud, they risk (4) _____. But things were slowly changing, more Americans began to recognize that freedom is a big part of what made us different from our (5) _____.

In case after case, the Supreme Court (6) _____ of all Americans to speak their minds, even if their views are (7) _____. Given this trend, the ruling in favor of the Westboro Baptist should come as no surprise. As justice Brandeis wrote way back in the 1920s: "When we were confronted with speech we don't agree with, the remedy to be applied is more speech ... (8) _____" it seems like the courts are more and more willing to give freedom the benefit of doubt and treat our First Amendment guarantees (9) _____.

Human Rights for Prisoners?

A. Decide whether the following statements are true or false.

[ ] 1. When speech is protected, democracy will benefit a lot.
[ ] 2. When a majority of people dislike us, our liberty is not protected by the Bill of Rights.
[ ] 3. We are ensured the right to have a lawyer under the Eighth Amendment.
[ ] 4. Clarens Gideon has been deprived of a fair trial because he has not been appointed a lawyer to represent him.

B. Fill in the blanks.

Or even people (1) _____ of crimes, people end up in a place like this. This is the old Tennessee (2) _____, it was built by prisoners in (3) _____ and closed just 20 years ago. It's empty now of course, but you can still feel what it was like. Interestingly enough, half of the amendments in the Bill of Rights are designed to protect people accused of crimes. But even though those rights are in the constitution itself, they are not guaranteed until (4) _____ and win them in the courts.

The supreme court agreed with him. Gideon was given a (5) _____, and the court appointed an attorney. This time it took the jury just one hour to acquit him. Since that landmark decision, anyone who is arrested, charged and facing prison time, is (6) _____, whether they are rich or poor, innocent or guilty.

Part IV Case Study and Speaking Task

MiAngel Cody, a Lawyer

A. Decide whether the following statements are true or false.

[ ] 1. Defendants are entitled the right of a fair trial by the constitution.

[ ] 2. The language used in the court room is not that incomprehensible to the defendant.

[ ] 3. Those who have admitted guilty in front of the lawyer should not be represented, according to MiAngel.

[ ] 4. The importance of locking a dangerous person up far outweighs the importance of his certain rights.

Lesson 9
Legal Concepts (1): Bill of Rights (US)

B. Fill in the blanks.

In the (1) _____ of Gideon, there were other landmark decisions, protecting the rights of the accused. The supreme court extended the (2) _____ by ruling that the suspects had to have an attorney present during interrogation. It revisited the Fourth Amendment, saying that physical evidence gathered without a (3) _____ cannot be used in court. Most famous of all was the Miranda case. The court took a fresh look at the Fifth Amendment protection against (4) _____. That decision gave birth to the familiar Miranda warning, "you have the right to (5) _____..."

C. Share your understanding with the class about your own idea of legal language.

Lesson 10

LEGAL CONCEPTS (2): EQUAL RIGHTS

Part I Getting Ready

The following words and phrases will appear in this unit. Use five minutes to find out the meanings of these words and phrases.

Listen carefully and study them.

1. Pinpoint
2. Ratification
3. Preamble
4. Matrimonial
5. Infringe
6. Bigotry
7. Short circuit
8. Immutable
9. Suffrage
10. Contraceptive

Lesson 10
Legal Concepts (2): Equal Rights

Part II Overview

A. Decide whether the following statements are true or false.

[ ] 1. Slavery is the basic contradiction at the heart of the constitution.

[ ] 2. The so-called radical Republicans of 1960s were supporters of slavery.

[ ] 3. Lincoln spearheaded the 13th Amendment to abolish slavery and remove the stain.

[ ] 4. "Dred Scott" decisions in 1875 are so destructive that it has to be undone.

B. Fill in the blanks.

In 1865, the country was emerging from the ashes of civil war, and it was time to deal with the constitutional problem that (1) _____ by the founding fathers-slavery. Most people have all these rights and liberties, and yet slaves have none. Slavery is this cancer in the constitution and it grows and grows, and eventually, the system breaks because of the (2) _____ .

With its (3) _____ , 4 million slaves were suddenly free. But that wouldn't be enough. No sooner had the war ended, the old regime of the south regained power, and passed laws to (4) _____ . The Republican would have to take extraordinary measures to ensure those rights, to (5) _____ that African Americans would be respected as citizens.

Part III Further Understanding

A. Decide whether the following statements are true or false.

[ ] 1. It was the 14th Amendment that merged the Declaration of Independence into the Constitution.

[ ] 2. African Americans had the voting rights after the Civil War.

[ ] 3. The Civil Rights Act of 1964 strengthened the 14th Amendment's guarantees of equality.

[ ] 4. Congress passed the Voting Rights Act to include all Americans in the democratic process in 1964.

B. Fill in the blanks.

For another century after the Civil War, state laws, especially in the South, kept millions of African Americans out of the (1) _____ with property and poll taxes, and (2) _____ in public places. Black citizens remained second-class citizens. For anyone who (3) _____ the rules, the penalties could be brutal. It would take a long struggle to overcome deeply-rooted racism, and rouse the (4) _____.

You might think that with all that struggle, the right to vote would today (5) _____, enjoyed by every American without exception. You'd be wrong.

C. Reorder the following sentences.

1. It would take a long struggle to overcome deeply-rooted racism, and rouse the conscience of the nation.

2. Thomas Jefferson's beautiful poetry about all men being created equal finally had the force of law.

Lesson 10
Legal Concepts (2): Equal Rights

3. But just because equality was now written into the Constitution which didn't make it real.

4. Today, the voting right is sacred and enjoyed by every American.

5. The Civil Rights Act of 1964 reinforced the 14th Amendment's guarantees of equality.

Reorder: _____

Part IV   Speaking Task

A. Decide whether the following statements are true or false.

[   ] 1. The 14th Amendment guarantees equal protection rights.

[   ] 2. Scholar Robert thinks that there is a fundamental problem with anti-miscegenation laws.

[   ] 3. Scholar Robert thinks that what we shouldn't do is to go into court and short circuit democratic process.

[   ] 4. History shows that our government has never drawn a clear distinction between different groups of people.

B. Fill in the blanks.

At the time, the state of Virginia had an (1) _____, banning inter-racial marriage. The lovings were found to be in violation of the law. They were ordered to leave the state or face a year in prison. The lovings sued the state of Virginia, and the Supreme Court ruled (2) _____. Under the constitution, the court held today (3) _____ that the freedom to marry or not marry a person of another race cannot be (4) _____ by racial discrimination.

It's true that sometimes, you have laws that's clearly (5) _____. We should be able to say that's true when that's true. But people who have conservative ideas about sex and marriage are not bigots. Now they can have a view, that's fine, they can compete for their view, and they can (6) _____ of their fellow citizens in a fair debate, then their view should (7) _____ . But people on the other side have exactly the same right.

The supreme court has ruled that because poverty is not what it called an (8) _____ , a permanent characteristic like race, equal protection clause doesn't provide much protection.

C. Answer the following questions.

1. What is the landmark case that linked marriage in the 14th Amendment?

2. What is the whole purpose of the 14th Amendment, according to Robert?

3. What's the purpose of the 19th Amendment?

4. What's so significant in 1971?

Lesson 10
Legal Concepts (2): Equal Rights

Part V Case Study

Interview with Michelle Alexander

Fill in the blanks.

The problem is, that we live in the era of (1) _____. You know, in the past few decades, we've quintupled our prison population. In the United States today if you have been labeled a criminal or a felon you are (2) _____ for many of the basic civil and human rights that were supposedly won in the civil rights movement and that so many of us take for granted. What you're doing is creating a new (3) _____. If we're going to be of, by, and for the people, it should include each and every one of us.

The words of the Constitution itself, (4) _____ that has yet to be fully fulfilled. It's not up to the lawyers and the judges alone, to make those words meaningful, it's up to all of us. If we want the 14th Amendment to guarantee (5) _____, it's going to take a movement of ordinary people defining what equal treatment really is.

Educational Rights for Illegal Immigrants

A. Discuss the following question.

The Lopez family came to America in illegal ways, including four kids. Should these kids receive the same education as American kids?

_____
_____
_____
_____
_____

B. Decide whether the following statements are true or false.

[ ] 1. It is estimated that around ten thousand illegal immigrants' children are at Texas schools.

[ ] 2. According to Texas laws, kids of illegal immigrants cannot receive education here.

[ ] 3. The Supreme Court rules that equal protections do not work here, since they are not Americans.

[ ] 4. The 14th Amendment is meant to provide equal rights for American citizens or those tax payers.

C. Fill in the blanks.

In Texas today (1) _____ begins in a federal court in a case challenging a state law that prohibits funding of education for the children of (2) _____. Their presence is becoming a major source of (3) _____.

Texas had just passed a law requiring that parents prove their kids were here legally, or pay (4) _____ for the (5) _____ of attending public school.

Everybody wants kids to get a good education. But if the 14th Amendment even made (6) _____ part of "We the People," where do we draw the line?

Interview with Professor Armar

Answer the following questions.

1. What is so significant about the 14th Amendment, according to the professor?

_____

_____

Lesson 10
Legal Concepts (2): Equal Rights

2. What is the use of the original and second version of the Bill of Rights?

_____

_____

3. Can we say that the 14th Amendment is enforcing a vision of liberty and justice for all?

_____

_____

Lesson 11

LEGAL CONCEPTS (3): CONSTITUTIONAL CRISIS

Part I   Getting Ready

The following words and phrases will appear in this unit. Use five minutes to find out the meanings of these words and phrases.

Listen carefully and study them.

1. Abide by
2. Makeover
3. Warranty
4. Ratify
5. Stall
6. Provision
7. Crook
8. Enter the fray
9. habeas corpus
10. Internment
11. Status quo

Lesson 11
Legal Concepts (3): Constitutional Crisis

Part II   Overview

The New Constitutional Construction in Iceland

Listen to the material, then fill in the blanks.

Welcome to Reykjavik, Iceland. This country of about (1) _____ people became an international financial capital during the boom years. Then in the crisis of 2008, everything (2) _____. The three largest banks collapsed. Parliament, which meets in that building over there, fell. (3) _____. Now, to keep anything like this from ever happening again, the people of Iceland, right now, (4) _____ creating and then approving a brand-new national constitution. They're throwing the old one out and starting again. The Icelanders took a real 21st century approach— inviting ordinary citizens to (5) _____ via Facebook and Twitter. Maybe they're on to something. Creating a new constitution, one that's (6) _____ for modern times.

The Development of the Constitution—Historian Rick Beeman

Listen to the interview with the professional on the development of the Constitution— historian Rick Beeman. Figure out whether the following statements are true or false.

[   ] 1. It is said that the Constitution has been in force for more than 225 years.

[   ] 2. According to Rick, the founding fathers of the Constitution would not be surprised that it has kept and developed in the same form.

[   ] 3. The founding fathers of the Constitution formed the framework which they wished to be flexible.

67

The Development of the Constitution—Professor Akhil Amar

A. Listen to the interview with the professional on the development of the Constitution—Professor Akhil Amar. Decide whether the following statements are true or false.

[ ] 1. According to Akhil, the founding fathers of the Constitution failed to reach an agreement on the degree of flexibility of the Constitution.

[ ] 2. Thomas Jefferson and James Madison had controversial views on the issue.

[ ] 3. Not every generation can revise the Constitution.

[ ] 4. Amendments to the Constitution will be quick to enact, or fail to pass.

B. Fill in the blanks.

One of the most amazing things about the Constitution is that (1) _____ after the last amendment. This is a deeply (2) _____ that there remains work for our generation to do.

The process is spelled out in (3) _____, and it's far from easy—it takes a (4) _____ of both houses, or a national convention, to propose amendments, then they have to be ratified by (5) _____. Over the past two centuries, thousands of amendments have been proposed, but only (6) _____ have actually been (7) _____. Amendments have addressed small things, like moving the date of presidential inaugurations.

Part III Further Understanding

Watergate Scandal

[Background] *Watergate was a major political scandal that occurred in the United States in the 1970s, following a break-in at the Democratic National Committee (DNC)*

Lesson 11
Legal Concepts (3): Constitutional Crisis

headquarters at the Watergate office complex in Washington, D.C. and President Richard Nixon's administration's attempted cover-up of its involvement. When the conspiracy was discovered and investigated by the U.S. Congress, the Nixon administration's resistance to its probes led to a constitutional crisis.

The term Watergate has come to encompass an array of clandestine and often illegal activities undertaken by members of the Nixon administration. Those activities included such "dirty tricks" as bugging the offices of political opponents and people of whom Nixon or his officials were suspicious. Nixon and his close aides ordered harassment of activist groups and political figures, using the Federal Bureau of Investigation (FBI), the Central Intelligence Agency (CIA), and the Internal Revenue Service (IRS).

The scandal led to the discovery of multiple abuses of power by the Nixon administration, articles of impeachment, and the resignation of Nixon as President of the United States in August 1974. The scandal also resulted in the indictment of 69 people, with trials or pleas resulting in 25 being found guilty and incarcerated, many of whom were Nixon's top administration officials.

A. Decide whether the following statements are true or false.

[ ] 1. Watergate Scandal began from the Presidential campaign of 1982.

[ ] 2. Among all the charges, Nixon had not ordered to record everything in the Oval Office.

[ ] 3. It is said that impeaching the President of the United States had never happened for more than 100 years.

[ ] 4. Nixon resigned, on August 9 two years later.

B. Fill in the blanks.

It's not (1) _____ in the text, but it was probably expected of us by our gentleman founders. You can call it good manners, or maybe respect. The executive has to respect the congress, but congress has to respect the (2) _____, and on around again, into a functioning government.

Nixon had not actually ordered the (3) _____, but he orchestrated a (4) _____. The Attorney General named a (5) _____. I welcome this kind of examination. Mr. Nixon has acted more like an imperial ruler. Lied repeatedly. (6) _____, or other high crimes and misdemeanors. Two branches of our government had reached an impasse. That's when the third branch, the Supreme Court, (7) _____, ruling that Nixon had to turn over the actual unedited tapes. House (8) _____ the President. Facing the certain prospect of removal from office, Nixon resigned, the first and so far only president to do so. So Watergate was a (9) _____.

C. Fill in the blanks.

So Watergate was a national trauma. But it was also a test. The Executive Branch (1) _____. Congress went to war with the President. The Supreme Court (2) _____ and Congress ended up removing a president from office, forcing him out. 187 years after it was written by men who never could have (3) _____ tape recorders or hidden microphones or televised hearings, the Constitution of the United States worked.

D. Answer the following questions.

1. Why did the impeachment on the president work?

   _____

   _____

2. Who will make the final call whenever disagreements come up?

   _____

   _____

Lesson 11
Legal Concepts (3): Constitutional Crisis

Anti-constitution During Wartime or Crisis

A. Decide whether the following statements are true or false.

[ ] 1. One of the reasons behind the longevity of the Constitution is that occasional repairs or amendments can be made.

[ ] 2. During wartime or crisis, Constitution cannot be sacrificed as a casualty.

[ ] 3. America mobilized to wage a new war against terrorism after the war.

[ ] 4. Americans called for Patriot Act after the nation was attacked.

B. Fill in the blanks.

Actually, the structure is a lot more (1) _____ than you might think. It all depends upon a (2) _____. And there are times when that balance just does not hold. In 1942, soon after the attack on Pearl Harbor, President Roosevelt issued an executive order that (3) _____ of more than 100,000 Japanese Americans, most of them American citizens. They were forced to abandon their homes and live in (4) _____ until the end of the war, even though there was little evidence they (5) _____ national security.

Patriot Act

A. Decide whether the following statements are true or false.

[ ] 1. It is the Patriot Act that gave the Administration authority to wiretap and surveillance.

[ ] 2. Adama Bah is one of the innocent people who were caught in a crackdown.

[ ] 3. Adama Bah knew clearly why she was being arrested and charged.

[ ] 4. It is Article III of the Constitution that has put the President in charge of the military.

B. Fill in the blanks.

There was bipartisan support in Congress, and the public, for expanding government powers to (1) _____, but many civil libertarians said the law (2) _____ the Constitution.

Adama was held in a Pennsylvania detention center, and (3) _____ frequent strip searches. After 6 weeks (4) _____, Adama was released. Adama Bah's story is (5) _____, but there were hundreds of reports of abuses against people detained as possible terrorists. Complaints of human rights (6) _____ continued throughout the Bush years, and beyond. President Obama (7) _____ too, for maintaining the indefinite detention of terrorism suspects, and for (8) _____ and targeted assassinations, including some aimed at American citizens.

Part IV　Speaking Task

Functions of the 9 Justices on the Supreme Court

Listen to the interview with former Justice Sandra Day O'Connor and provide answer to these questions.

1. What are the guiding principles for the judges to make decisions?

   _____

   _____

2. Should the judges put a lot of weight into what's called original intent?

   _____

   _____

Lesson 11
Legal Concepts (3): Constitutional Crisis

Part V Case Study

Interview with Rabbi Douglas Sagal

Listen to the interview with Rabbi Douglas Sagal and fill in the blanks.

I know, your job is to interpret this (1) _____ text written on animal skin, for (2) _____ people who live in modern New Jersey. That's a full-time job and sometimes very stressful. Is there anything that you have learned doing this that you think you could offer an advice to those people who (3) _____ trying to apply a 225-year-old document to life in these modern United States? Well, in my own view, the Constitution is (4) _____ . I believe, I could be wrong, that the founders intended for it to be a living document just as the Torah is a living document.

Interview with Professor Amar

Fill in the blanks.

Why has it endured? I mean, there are (1) _____ times change. It's been two and a half centuries, almost. Why do you think we've kept it the same way? Because the people keep (2) _____ . So it's the "We the people," this idea—it's an intergenerational idea. It's about (3) _____ , and generation after generation has joined the game and been willing to play it. I'd want us to remember this document, this Constitution isn't just about (4) _____ . But what has been happening every day since and what is still happening. Because it's this epic... (5) _____ ... conversation over two centuries and it's still continuing. And it's more perfect than what came before, and it's the job of our generation to make it more perfect still.

Lesson 12

LEGAL CONCEPTS (4): PRESUMED INNOCENT

Part I   Getting Ready

The following words and phrases will appear in this unit. Use five minutes to find out the meanings of these words and phrases.

Listen carefully and study them.

1. Escort
2. Aberration
3. Disproportionate
4. Miscarriage
5. Enshrine
6. Seismic
7. Forgery
8. Medieval
9. Forensic
10. Deter
11. Exemplary
12. Rampage

Lesson 12
Legal Concepts (4): Presumed Innocent

Part II Overview

Listen to the passage on fair trial and answer the following questions.

1. What has happened to John Smith?

   _____

   _____

2. Why does the passage say that such disproportionate punishment was no miscarriage of justice?

   _____

   _____

3. That transformation was shaped by (1) _____ in English society "from the (2) _____" to the rise of the popular press.

Development of Lawyer's Role—Garrow's Contribution

A. Decide whether the following statements are true or false.

[ ] 1. It is said that the juries were considerably less punitive 200 years ago than what we might think.

[ ] 2. Counting on the mercy of either the jury or the judge could seem a little bit like Russian Roulette.

[ ] 3. From the listening we know that lawyers started serving in English courts since the 15th century, but their roles were limited to civil cases and litigation.

[ ] 4. It is said that defense barristers could address the jury directly with cross-examination.

B. Fill in the blanks.

By the 18th century, barristers were (1) _____ on behalf of the Crown. "And from the 1730s, some judges were allowing defence barristers to appear on behalf of prisoners (2) _____." Barristers appearing in criminal cases couldn't fall back on mere rhetoric. They had to master a forensic (3) _____. Since the 13th century, it was not considered proper for a barrister, in effect, to appear against the King (4) _____ that were brought by the crown.

The son of a Scottish schoolmaster, Garrow was called to the bar in (5) _____. In later life he would become an MP, the Attorney General and a Privy Councillor, but his lasting impact came from the time he spent at the Old Bailey as one of the most (6) _____ of his era.

C. Listen again and fill in the missing information based on what you have heard.

Garrow may have been a mould-breaker in the courtroom, but he was also very much (1) _____ the mindset of his age. In 18th-century Britain, the prevailing intellectual climate was one of (2) _____, even of skepticism. Learned institutions such as the Royal Society championed and popularised the scientific method. The instinct of any educated person of Garrow's generation would be to (3) _____, but to question received wisdom and to test the evidence. "And this Enlightenment thinking had found its way into the courtroom." Previously, all evidence, even (4) _____, "but now rules of what could and could not be considered evidence were introduced."

The trial was no longer (5) _____, but of the evidence against him. And linked to this approach is a principle that has become the cornerstone of ideals of justice across the world, yet can be summed up in one phrase. Innocent until (6) _____.

Lesson 12
Legal Concepts (4): Presumed Innocent

Part III Further Understanding

Robert Peel's Contribution to Forgery

Listen to the tape and write down what you have heard.

_____
_____
_____
_____
_____
_____

Interview with Lord Hurd on Robert Peel's Reform

A. Decide whether the following statements are true or false.

[ ] 1. It is said that over the previous 100 years, there had been a vast amount of Parliamentary legislation dealing with crimes.

[ ] 2. Roughly speaking, there is around 140 acts to do with forgery, among which 60 created capital offences.

[ ] 3. According to Lord Hurd, Peel was not a humanitarian, just a liberal Home Secretary.

[ ] 4. The real purpose of Peel is to make things sensible and tidy, for the system.

B. Answer the following questions.

1. What has happened in August, 2011?

   _____
   _____

2. Why did Peel advocate the creation of a police force?

   _____
   _____

3. Why were people at that time opposing to the idea of creating police forces?

   _____
   _____

C. Fill in the blanks.

Instead of (1) _____ and employing water cannon, "governments relied on the Riot Act." The Act held that where 12 or more people gathered together in riotous assembly and rejected the reading of the Riot Act and failed to (2) _____, then force could be used against them. Those remaining on the scene would be subject to the most severe penalty of all -(3) _____.

In (4) _____, he did this by persuading the public that the police would not just control people, they would primarily (5) _____. Crucially for English criminal law, the creation of a professional police force meant they became the (6) _____ rather than (7) _____.

Lesson 12
Legal Concepts (4): Presumed Innocent

Part IV Speaking Task

A. Answer the following questions.

1. What is the only means of deterring crime in the 18th century?

2. Is it true that because of the Waltham Blacks, every offence was punished by death?

3. What has happened to The Old Bailey in 1750 that made it a death trap?

4. If the defendant needed assistance, will the judge help?

5. How many crimes has Bloody Code sanctioning hanged?

B. Fill in the blanks.

No. And you were lucky if the entire proceedings (1) _____ and sentence took more than 15 minutes. The idea that the accused (2) _____ an adequate defense had yet to penetrate these walls. Many an accused, when compelled to defend themselves in this alien environment, with its (3) _____, would have been terrified into incoherence when their lives were hanging in the balance.

Spencer Cowper, grandfather of the poet William, was on trial for murder. Towards the end of a (4) _____, an exhausted judge admitted he was struggling to sum up the case. "I am sensible and I have omitted many things," he said, "but I am a little faint and cannot repeat any more of the evidence." Despite this display of (5) _____, or perhaps because of it, the jury found Cowper not guilty.

C. Retell the story in your own words to the class.

Lesson 13
LAYING DOWN THE LAW—ENGLISH COMMON LAW

Part I Getting Ready

The following words and phrases will appear in this unit. Use five minutes to find out the meanings of these words and phrases.

Listen carefully and study them.

1. Wig
2. Embody
3. Forge
4. Barrister
5. Chaplain
6. Venerable

Part II Overview

A. Answer the following questions.

1. What is the danger of this legal establishment on show, according to the listening?

_____

_____

2. Who has been the centre of the legal system for centuries?

_____
_____

3. Who have put law back in its path of justice and fairness?

_____
_____

B. Fill in the blanks.

Without (1) _____ in history, English law came to embody a (2) _____ barely known elsewhere. In this series, I'll show how the story of England's law is nothing less than the story of (3) _____. I'll explain how despite (4) _____ by kings and invaders, "by the Church and politicians, English law has always resisted" becoming merely the tool of the powerful. "But this isn't an open and shut case." The law has also been (5) _____. Its methods have sometimes been merciless. The result, in my opinion, (6) _____ anything England has achieved in the arts or the sciences.

The Origin of the English Common Law

A. Fill in the blanks.

I've come to Rochester in Kent to (1) _____ the earliest-known English law code. Established in the (2) _____ century, Kent is thought to have been the first (3) _____. Rochester's ancient cathedral and imposing castle (4) _____ to the region's early predominance. Stored in the council archives is a book of (5) _____, not just for the law but for the entire English-speaking world. It contains a number of documents but the most significant is the first, and it's this. A few pages of a text (6) _____. It's not only the first writing in English that we have, also it's the (7) _____, it's the first law code that we

Lesson 13
Laying Down the Law—English Common Law

have. It's a very simple list of fines or compensation for accidents, (8) _____ .

B. Listen to this passage and answer the following questions.

1. How many different ranks have been mentioned in the interview, and what are they?

   _____

   _____

2. Who determines the amount of compensation that they are entitled to?

   _____

   _____

3. Who has the responsibility for enforcing laws?

   _____

   _____

C. Fill in the blanks.

The clear categories and prices of Aethelberht's code (1) _____ this Anglo-Saxon subjects, whose economy centred around farming and livestock rearing. At 40, four... Still, a law code (2) _____ cost appears morally rather empty. But in the context of the time, it had much merit. The ability to (3) _____, to (4) _____, was crucial in the early Anglo-Saxon era when the greatest threat to the stability of society came not from external enemies but from (5) _____. Before the Royal regulation of law, blood feuds were the only form of justice available in Anglo-Saxon lands, and they could lead to (6) _____ that threatened the entire realm.

Part III Further Understanding

The Vicissitude of Law

Answer the following questions.

1. What is the next step after admitting laws being the essential basis of legal system?

2. Which part could deal with serious disputes and crimes?

3. What were early trials based on?

4. How many oath helpers did you need to depend on?

5. How many people were required in a case of arson or murder?

The Later Anglo-Saxons Age

Answer the following questions.

1. What was a clear way of preventing crime?

Lesson 13
Laying Down the Law—English Common Law

2. What additional method has been adopted in the later Anglo-Saxons age?

3. What were the main kinds of ordeal employed in England?

4. What is the meaning of sinking and floating respectively?

Interview with Professor John Hudson

Answer the following questions.

1. What factors determined "whether you were sent for ordeal in the first place"?

2. What is the real purpose of ordeals?

3. How many people had got off the ordeal for the 13th century?

4. What are the convincing factors after suspects carrying a hot iron?

5. Who has the greatest control over the ordeal process?

The End of Anglo-Saxons Age; Norman Empire

A. Decide whether the following statements are true or false.

[   ] 1. The most important principle for any ruler of England is to go with rather than against "the grain of the law."

[   ] 2. William invaded England because of his greed for bigger empire.

[   ] 3. Norman allowed the people to pursue their Anglo-Saxon legal traditions because they believed that was the best way to rule the country.

[   ] 4. It was Henry II who came to the throne in 1145 that sorted out the mass.

B. Answer the questions.

1. When did England suffer from what was called "The Anarchy" and "the 19-Year Winter"?

   _____

   _____

2. What did historians call Henry II?

   _____

   _____

3. What is the purpose of Justices traveling around the country?

   _____

   _____

C. Fill in the blanks.

Henry realised that it wasn't sufficient just to issue laws. The trick was to (1) _____. So in 1166, Henry established a system of (2) _____. These (3) _____ represented a new level of intervention by the Crown in English law. The Justices were to travel the country. The Justices weren't mere functionaries. The first pair to set off included one of his chief ministers and the

Lesson 13
Laying Down the Law—English Common Law

(4) _____ of Essex. They managed to get as far as Carlisle when the Earl rather inconveniently fell ill and died. Before his (5) _____, in the space of just a few months, they'd managed to (6) _____ half the shires of England.

Part IV Speaking Task

Establishment of the Great Charter, Magna Carta

A. Answer the following questions.

1. What is supposed to happen on 15th June, 1215?

   _____
   _____

2. What has the king done to alienate England's powerful barons?

   _____
   _____

3. What is the meaning of the Great Charter?

   _____
   _____

4. What has the Great Charter been hailed as?

   _____
   _____

B. Share your own understanding with your partner on the Great Charter.

Lesson 14

THE PURSUIT OF LIBERTY—ENGLISH COMMON LAW

Part I   Getting Ready

The following words and phrases will appear in this unit. Use five minutes to find out the meanings of these words and phrases.

Listen carefully and study them.

1. Induce
2. Conspirator
3. Rack
4. Barbarous
5. Arbitrary
6. Come to a head
7. Abolition
8. Shoplifting
9. Pledge
10. Prerogative
11. By-word
12. Inception
13. Come to the fore
14. Mafia

Lesson 14
The Pursuit of Liberty—English Common Law

Part II Overview

Listen to the passage and answer the following questions.

1. What is the exact time that the mob attacked the palace in a protest against the king?

2. What was the reason that Archer had been charged?

3. Was Archer the last one to be tortured in England?

4. Why was the 17th-century equivalent of Guantanamo Bay so special?

Star Chamber

Fill in the blanks.

One of the most satisfying, and challenging, aspects of my job as a criminal defence barrister is (1) _____. Any trial has to be held in a court open to the public, before an independent jury, and by a judge who is pledged "to (2) _____," "beholden to no master other than the law." But in the years leading up to the Civil War, England had a two-tier legal system. (3) _____, and a system under the (4) _____, which allowed torture, and enabled the King to do as he saw fit.

The nobility seems (5) _____. They can intimidate juries and bribe judges. So the Crown develops a court. It has powers that can tame the English Mafia. Justice was dispensed under this ceiling of gold stars, from which the court gets its name — Star Chamber. It had no jury that could be (6) _____ by the mighty. Instead, errant aristocrats were (7) _____, by members of the government itself. A bit like being tried by Kenneth Clarke.

Corrupted Star Chamber

Decide whether the following statements are true or false.

[ ] 1. Once a court controled lawless nobles, Star Chamber has become a threat to people.

[ ] 2. In order to get money, the King ordered thousands of soldiers to forcibly garrison people's homes across the country.

[ ] 3. According to the passage, seven of Charles' knights were imprisoned without trial for refusing to pay.

[ ] 4. It was Edward Coke, 76-year-old veteran of the Star Chamber, that finally stood out.

Part III Further Understanding

Petition of Right

Decide whether the following statements are true or false.

[ ] 1. We can only say that the significance of the draft by Edward Coke is second only to that of Magna Carta.

Lesson 14
The Pursuit of Liberty—English Common Law

[ ] 2. Even if the Petition of Rights is only two pages long, it has changed the course of history.

[ ] 3. Majesty's courts have denied the petition once after seeding it.

[ ] 4. According to the passage, the jailer should justify their actions to the prisoners if they ask for it.

[ ] 5. It is said that the Petition of Rights is not just significant in 18th-century England, but also one of the foundation documents of civil liberties.

Petition's Crisis

Fill in the blanks.

Across England, the agreement of Charles to this document was welcomed by the ringing of church bells and the (1) _____. A rare event for a parliamentary measure. But the celebrations had barely died down before Charles was (2) _____. Once he had secured his cash, the King bypassed the Petition of Right and (3) _____ Parliament. He would rule alone, enforcing his will through the court of Star Chamber. The Star Chamber judges (4) _____ an alternative form of taxation, by fining the wealthy on frivolous charges. And Charles, a man who saw opposition everywhere, could also use Star Chamber, and its savage sentences, to (5) _____ on religious, as well as political, (6) _____.

Part IV Speaking Task

Fighting for Power—King vs. Parliament

Answer the following questions.

1. What is one of the reasons for the Civil War, according to the listening?

2. Who won in the end and how many have been sacrificed during the war?

3. How did criminal barristers get their cases?

4. Barristers can't choose which case they take on. What is this called?

Part V Research and Presentation

You and your partners are supposed to work as a team, and to find out some resources to give a presentation in plain language to explain the English Common Law System. Try to manage your time in five minutes.

Lesson 15
INTERNATIONAL BUSINESS LAW

Part I Getting Ready

The following words and phrases will appear in this unit. Use five minutes to find out the meanings of these words and phrases.

Listen carefully and study them.

1. International law
2. Public international law
3. Private international law
4. Jurisdiction
5. Judicial decisions
6. International business law
7. Customary law
8. Common law
9. Civil law
10. Comity
11. Precedent
12. General principles of law
13. Conventions and treaties
14. Adversarial procedure
15. Inquisitorial procedure

Part II Overview

A. Write down their Chinese equivalents.

1. bench _____   2. party _____   3. order _____

4. bar _____   5. forum _____   6. consideration _____

7. instrument _____ 8. save _____   9. hearing _____

B. Tick the answers that you think are the right.

1. Which international relationships do the international law deal with?

   (　) a. those between states and states

   (　) b. those between states and persons

   (　) c. those between persons and persons

2. Which of the followings are the main contents of public international law?

   (　) a. sources of international law

   (　) b. scope of international law

   (　) c. international personality

   (　) d. state territory

   (　) e. state succession

   (　) f. law of the sea

   (　) g. international dispute settlement

   (　) h. torts

   (　) i. marriage and divorce

3. Which of the followings are the main contents of international business law?

   (　) a. international trade law

   (　) b. contract law

   (　) c. agency law

( ) d. product liability law

( ) e. corporate law

( ) f. partnership law

( ) g. international investment law

( ) h. intellectual property law

( ) i. property law

Part III Further Understanding

International Law

A. You are going to hear the statement about the introduction of international law. Fill in the blanks with the words you have heard in the following passage after the first listening.

International law is, however, more than just good manners or mutual respect between or among sovereign nation-states. Comity, for example, is the practice between states of treating each other with goodwill and civility.

International law is the body of (1)_____ that regulates activities carried on (2)_____ the legal boundaries of a single state.

International law falls into (3)_____ international law and (4)_____ international law.

Private international law deals with the rights and duties of (5)_____ and (6)_____ organizations in their international affairs.

Public international law should not be (7)_____ "private international law," which is concerned with the resolution of (8)_____ .

Comity, for example, is the practice between states of treating each other with (9)_____ and (10)_____.

B. You are going to hear the statement for the second time. Answer the following questions after listening.

1. Is international law really law?
   _____
   _____

2. Has the subject matter of international law changed dramatically in recent years?
   _____
   _____

3. Is comity really law?
   _____
   _____

What Is International Business Law?

You are going to hear the statement about the introduction of international business law. Have a dictation of the description. You will hear the recording three times.

_____
_____
_____
_____
_____

Lesson 15
International Business Law

Part IV   Watching and Speaking

What Are the Sources of International Law?

Watch the video and then discuss with your partner about the sources of International Law. Share your opinion with the class.

What Is Common Law? What Are the Differences Between Civil Law and Common Law?

Watch the video and then discuss with your partner about what common law and the differences between civil law and common law is. Share your opinion with the class.

Part V   Research and Presentation

Divide into groups, and try to interview some people about the following questions. Note down their answers and then make a presentation in class to introduce your findings.

1. What are the differences between international law and domestic law?

   _____

   _____

2. Can you distinguish the treaties from the conventions?

   _____

   _____

3. What is the customary law? How can we judge that a customary practice has become customary law?

_____

_____

4. Can you make a list of the organs of the United Nations?

_____

_____

5. Please tell us an important intergovernmental organization. And give us a brief introduction.

_____

_____

6. How does international law look upon individuals?

_____

_____

Part VI Case Study

Commission of the European Communities brought suit for a declaration that Germany's Meat Regulation, prohibiting the importation and "marketing of meat products which contain ingredients other than meat," fails to fulfill Germany's obligation under Article 30 of the EEC Treaty.

Do any of the justifications advanced by Germany allow the Meat Regulation to be upheld as a valid restraint on trade?

Lesson 16
BUSINESS ORGANIZATION LAW

Part I Getting Ready

The following words and phrases will appear in this unit. Use five minutes to find out the meanings of these words and phrases.

Listen carefully and study them.

1. Business Enterprise
2. Board of directors
3. Corporate governance
4. Juristic person
5. Articles of incorporation
6. Pierce the corporate veil
7. Commission
8. Liquidation
9. Publicly held corporation
10. Closely held corporation
11. Subsidiary
12. Representative office
13. International multinationals
14. International business agent
15. Foreign distributorship

Part II Overview

A. If you would like to set up a business, what factors do you think you need to take into consideration? Write down your answers in the table and compare them with your partner's.

B. The following are some commonly-used legal business organizations. Choose the right words from the box below to fill in the blanks. If you would like to set up a business, which of the following business organizations do you prefer? Give your reasons.

sole proprietorship, general partnership, limited partnership, corporation, nonprofit corporation, limited liability company, joint venture, franchise

1. A _____ is the simplest type of business entity owned and run by a single person. The owner is personally liable for all the debts of the business.

2. A _____ is a form of entity business created by agreement in which 2 or more co-owners engage in business for profit. Each one agrees to contribute money, labor, or skill to a business.

3. A _____ is a partnership formed by 2 or more persons or entities, having one or more general partners and one or more limited partners. The limited partners typically are not involved in daily running of the business.

4. A _____ is a business enterprise that offers the limited liability of a corporation and the tax advantages of a partnership.

5. A _____ is one that is organized for charitable or benevolent purposes. It includes hospitals, homes and universities.

6. A _____ is an artificial being, existing in law only and neither tangible nor visible. As a legal entity, it has rights and liabilities that are separate and distinct from those of its shareholders.

7. A _____ is a method of starting a business which minimizes risk by using or emulating a tried and tested "business formula."

8. A _____ is a business entity created by two or more parties, generally characterized by shared ownership, shared returns and risks, and shared governance.

Part III Further Understanding

A. Fill in the blanks after the first listening.

1. They both are separate _____ that will take liability away from the business owner and place it on the new legal entity in the event of _____.

2. Limited liability companies serve _____ of the clients the best, simply because there is a lot _____ on a yearly basis to deal with in the simple fact you can always convert a limited liability company to a corporation.

3. One of the greatest features of a corporation is the ability to _____ to investors, also known as _____.

4. There are also two forms of corporation, which are the _____ and the _____.

5. An S corporation basically allows you to _____ your tax return, meaning you could put your corporate taxes directly on your _____.

B. You are going to hear the statement the second time, answer questions after listening.

1. If your company is never going to have over 50 employees or you're never planning on going public with it or you don't want to sell shares to different people for fund-raising, why will a limited liability company be most likely the best choice for you?
   _____
   _____

2. Why are corporations more complicated?
   _____
   _____

3. Are corporations valuable if you plan in the future on trading your company on the stock exchange?
   _____
   _____

How Is a Corporation Like a Person?

Have a dictation of the description. You will hear the recording three times.

_____
_____
_____
_____
_____
_____

Lesson 16
Business Organization Law

Part IV Watching and Speaking

Piercing the Corporate Veil

Watch the video and then discuss with your partner about your understanding of piercing the corporate veil. Share your opinion with the class.

What Is a Multinational Corporation?

Watch the video and then discuss with your partner about the introduction of multinational corporation. Share your opinion with the class.

Part V Research and Presentation

Divide into groups, and try to interview some people about the following questions. Note down their answers and then make a presentation in class to introduce your findings.

1. What are the characteristics of sole proprietorship?

   _____

   _____

2. What are the contents of partnership agreements?

   _____

   _____

3. What are the internal and external relationship of a partnership?

   _____

   _____

4. What is the difference between branch and subsidiary?

5. What is the difference between agent and representative office?

6. What are the considerations when buying a franchise?

Part VI Case Study

Dow Jones published *Barron's* Online, whose October 28, 2000 edition had an article which made several statements about Joe Gutnick, a resident of Australia. Although only five copies of the print edition went from the U.S. to Australia, the Internet version had 1700 online subscribers in Australia, out of over 500,000 worldwide. Mr. Gutnick sued Dow Jones in Australia for defamation. The trial and appellate courts both found that Australian courts had personal jurisdiction over Dow Jones.

Do the Australian courts have personal jurisdiction over Dow Jones & Co.?

Lesson 17
INTERNATIONAL COMMERCIAL ARBITRATION

Part I Getting Ready

The following words and phrases will appear in this unit. Use five minutes to find out the meanings of these words and phrases.

Listen carefully and study them.

1. Commence the arbitration
2. Advisory
3. Arbitral award
4. Binding
5. Enforceable
6. Expedient
7. Final
8. Alternative dispute resolution
9. Arbitral tribunal
10. International commercial arbitration
11. Impartial
12. Ad hoc arbitration
13. Ad hoc committee
14. Null and void
15. New York Convention

Part II Overview

A. Do you know what ADR stands for? Tick the following forms which you think are of ADR processes.

( ) 1. arbitration   ( ) 2. mediation

( ) 3. neutral education   ( ) 4. mini-trials

( ) 5. good offices   ( ) 6. negotiation

( ) 7. settlement conferences   ( ) 8. private judging

( ) 9. hybrids of these processes   ( ) 10. conciliation

B. What requirements shall the persons who request arbitration meet?

_____

_____

Part III Further Understanding

A. Fill in the blanks with the words you have heard in the following passage after the first listening.

An arbitration is the settlement of a dispute after a (1)_____ of opposing arguments, by an (2)_____, rather than a court of law. If binding arbitration is accepted, the parties involved agree to follow the arbitrator's (3)_____, which is binding only on the parties to the dispute, and is not a legal (4)_____, as is a judicial ruling.

Different with mediation and (5)_____, arbitration results in a binding and

Lesson 17
International Commercial Arbitration

(6)_____ award. A conciliator cannot (7)_____ the parties to reach a settlement and a conciliator has no power to (8)_____ on the parties.

In this time of market (9)_____, many industrial companies are including detailed (10)_____ in their international contracts.

B. You are going to hear the statement the second time. Answer the following questions after listening.

1. What's the difference between an arbitration and a trial?
   _____
   _____

2. Compared with mediation and conciliation, what is the advantage of arbitration? Explain it in your own words.
   _____
   _____

3. Why do so many industrial companies write detailed arbitration clauses in their international contracts?
   _____
   _____

Advantages of Arbitration

You are going to hear the statement about the advantages of arbitration. Have a dictation of the description. You will hear the recording three times.

_____
_____
_____
_____

Part IV Watching and Speaking

International Arbitration

Watch the video and then discuss with your partner about your understanding of international arbitration, and share your opinion with the class.

International Commercial Arbitration Explained

Watch the video and then discuss with your partner about the introduction of international commercial arbitration, and share your opinion with the class.

Part V Research and Presentation

Divide into groups, and try to interview some people about the following questions. Note down their answers and then make a presentation in class to introduce your findings.

1. Can you introduce some main domestic and international arbitration institutions?

   _____
   _____

2. Can you introduce the basic types of arbitration agreement?

   _____
   _____

3. What are the functions of arbitration agreement?

   _____
   _____

Lesson 17
International Commercial Arbitration

4. What are the main contents of arbitration clauses?

5. How does the Arbitration Process work?

6. What are the grounds for challenging an award?

Part VI   Case Study

A Mississippi, US businessman sued Canada-based funeral conglomerate The Loewen Group (Loewen) in state court for breach of contract. The jury returned various verdicts totaling US $500 million. Loewen wanted to appeal without posting a bond for 125% of damages; appeal bonds are a standard practice in US state courts. The Mississippi Supreme Court rejected Loewen's motion, so it settled with plaintiff for US $150 million, 30% of the jury verdict. In October 1998, Loewen filed suit against the US in ICSID under NAFTA Article 11, arguing that the punitive damages and appeal bond requirement violated its rights as an investor. Loewen asked for $725 million in compensation from the US government.

Did the Mississippi court proceedings violate US obligations under NAFTA Article 11?

Lesson 18
THE DISPUTE SETTLEMENT SYSTEM OF WTO

Part I   Getting Ready

The following words and phrases will appear in this unit. Use five minutes to find out the meanings of these words and phrases.

Listen carefully and study them.

1. Reconcile
2. Conciliation
3. Mediation
4. Arbitration
5. DSB
6. DSU
7. Appellate Body
8. Appellate Review
9. Panelist
10. Enforcement
11. Precedential
12. Concession
13. Expertise
14. Discretion
15. Exclusive jurisdiction

Lesson 18
The Dispute Settlement System of WTO

Part II Overview

A. The following statements are related with the functions, objectives and key features of the dispute settlement system. Write down which statements are true and which are false.

> (1) Providing security and predictability to the multilateral trading system
>
> (2) Preserving the rights and obligations of WTO Members
>
> (3) Clarification of rights and obligations through interpretation
>
> (4) "Mutually Agreed Solutions" as "Preferred Solution"
>
> (5) Private individuals or companies have direct access to the dispute settlement system
>
> (6) Prohibition against unilateral determinations
>
> (7) Exclusive jurisdiction
>
> (8) Compulsory nature
>
> (9) Prompt settlement of disputes
>
> (10) Normally appeals should not last more than 30 days, with an absolute maximum of 60 days.

B. What are the settlements of disputes in the International Tribunals?

_____

_____

Part III Listening and Speaking

A. Fill in the blanks.

The WTO is responsible or (1)_____ and (2)_____ the rules of international trade between nations.

1. The Dispute Settlement Panels is made up of three (3)_____ from states not (4)_____ in the dispute.

3. The panel (5)_____ may be appealed to (6)_____ by a party to the dispute.

4. Member states are encouraged to (7)_____ disputes with each other by (8)_____.

5. And if both parties agree, they may seek the (9)_____ of third parties in conducting (10)_____ about their dispute.

B. You are going to hear the statement the second time. Answer questions orally after listening.

1. What is the function of WTO?

2. What organs does DSU have?

3. What is the function of the Dispute Settlement Panels?

Lesson 18
The Dispute Settlement System of WTO

The Dispute Settlement Understanding

You are going to hear the statement about the dispute settlement understanding. Have a dictation of the description. You will hear the recording three times.

_____
_____
_____
_____
_____
_____

Part IV Watching and Speaking

GATT and WTO — Social Studies

Watch the video and then discuss with your partner about your understanding of GATT and WTO — Social Studies. Share your opinion with the class.

WTO Accused of Failing to Assist Developing Nations

Watch the video and then discuss with your partner about the accusation on WTO. Share your opinion with the class.

Part V Research and Presentation

Divide into groups, and try to interview some people about the following questions. Note down their answers and then make a presentation in class to introduce your findings.

1. What are the legal natures of WTO DSU?

2. How many panelists are there in the Dispute Settlement Body?

3. What are the responsibilities of the Dispute Settlement Body?

4. How many persons are there in the Appellate Body?

5. Can you list some famous WTO agreements?

6. Do the rulings of the Panel and Appellate Body have precedential effect?

Lesson 18
The Dispute Settlement System of WTO

Part VI Case Study

The EC, Canada, and the US complained that Japan's application of its Liquor Tax Law did not comply with the requirements of GATT. The WTO Panel hearing the complaint concluded, among other things, that "panel reports adopted by the [old] GATT [1947] Contracting Parties and the [new] WTO Dispute Settlement Bodies" constitute "subsequent practice" that were to be treated as "an integral part of GATT 1994." In other words, they were to be regarded as precedents. On the appeal of this case, the US argued that the Panel hearing the case had erred in making this finding.

Must the panel reports adopted by the GATT 1947 Contracting Parties be treated as precedents?

Lesson 19
INTERNATIONAL CENTER FOR SETTLEMENT OF INVESTMENT DISPUTES

Part I   Getting Ready

The following words and phrases will appear in this unit. Use five minutes to find out the meanings of these words and phrases.

Listen carefully and study them.

1. International Bank for Reconstruction and Development
2. Administrative Council
3. Secretariat
4. Panel of Arbitrators
5. Panel of Conciliators
6. Secretary-general
7. Mitigate
8. Registrar
9. Intervene
10. Host state
11. Home state
12. Waive
13. Unilateral withdrawal

Lesson 19
International Center for Settlement of Investment Disputes

14. Washington Convention
15. Exclusive Remedy

Part II Overview

A. When was the World Bank Group established? What is the purpose of the World Bank?

_____

_____

B. List the five agencies of the World Bank Group.

_____

_____

Part III Listening and Speaking

A. Fill in the blanks with the words you have heard in the following sentences after the first listening.

1. The International Centre for Settlement of Investment Disputes (ICSID) is an _____ institution established in 1966 for legal dispute resolution and _____ between international investors.

2. As of 2014 there were _____ member countries contracting with and _____ the ICSID.

3. The council chooses the _____ and the _____ from nominees submitted by states parties.

4. The Secretariat, made up of a _____ and an administrative staff, serves as the ICSID's legal representative, _____ and principal officer.

5. ICSID has encouraged the development of a larger and more _____ group of case _____, who reflect the diversity of ICSID's membership.

B. You are going to hear the statement the second time. Answer questions after listening.

1. What is the purpose of the establishment of ICSID?
   _____
   _____

2. What organs does ICSID have?
   _____
   _____

3. What is the most important basic rule established by the Washington Convention?
   _____
   _____

Constituting an ICSID Arbitration Tribunal

You are going to hear the statement about constituting an ICSID arbitration tribunal. Have a dictation of the description. You will hear the recording three times.

_____
_____
_____
_____
_____
_____

Lesson 19
International Center for Settlement of Investment Disputes

Part IV   Watching and Speaking

Investment Arbitration

Watch the video and then discuss with your partner about your understanding of investment arbitration, and share your opinion with the class.

The Importance of Diversity in Investment Arbitration

Watch the video and then discuss with your partner about the importance of diversity in investment arbitration, and share your opinion with the class.

Part V   Research and Presentation

Divide into groups, and try to interview some people about the following questions. Note down their answers and then make a presentation in class to introduce your findings.

1. What's the situation where ICSID has jurisdiction?

   _____

   _____

2. What is the exclusive remedy?

   _____

   _____

3. Who may serve as an arbitrator, conciliator or ad hoc Committee member in ICSID proceedings?

_____

_____

4. How many arbitrators can be selected for the litigation in ICSID?

_____

_____

5. What are the major functions of IBRD, IFC, IDA, MIGA, ICSID in the World Bank Group?

_____

_____

6. How are the procedural languages selected by the parties?

_____

_____

Part VI   Case Study

Plaintiff, State C. Cee. Co asks ICSID to convene an arbitration tribunal. Plaintiff set up a subsidiary in defendant's territory. And defendant promised plaintiff a tax holiday for twenty years, but plaintiff required defendant to sign an ICSID arbitration agreement. The government of defendant has changed, and the new government has cancelled all tax holiday granted to foreign firms, including plaintiff. Defendant informed ICSID that it no longer considers disputes relating to taxes as being arbitrable.

Does the tribunal have jurisdiction to proceed?

Lesson 20

PROTECTION OF INTELLECTUAL PROPERTY

Part I Getting Ready

The following words and phrases will appear in this unit. Use five minutes to find out the meanings of these words and phrases.

Listen carefully and study them.

1. Piracy
2. An exclusive right
3. Collective marks
4. Patented inventions
5. Unauthorized copying
6. A fair use defense
7. Copyright Act
8. Original work of authorship
9. Patent Act
10. Suits for infringement
11. Under the authority of
12. Right of priority
13. Compulsory license
14. Registered trademark
15. Principle of reciprocity

Part II Overview

A. Match the following Chinese terms related to intellectual property with their English equivalents by drawing lines between them.

1. 专利   a. copyright
2. 工业产权   b. industrial property
3. 著作权   c. trademarks
4. 工业品外观设计   d. patent
5. 盗版产品   e. infringement
6. 专属权   f. industrial designs
7. 商标   g. commercial exploitation
8. 侵权   h. exclusive right
9. 版税   i. royalties
10. 商业性利用   j. pirated goods

B. Publishers and lawyers like to describe copyright as "intellectual property." Actually, it is a term much broader than that. Work in pairs talking about more examples of the infringement of intellectual property in our everyday life.

_____

_____

Lesson 20
Protection of Intellectual Property

Part III Listening and Speaking

What Is Intellectual Property?

A. Fill in the blanks with the words you have heard in the following sentences after the first time.

1. Intellectual property usually refers to a range of _____, which is a collection of ideas and information in a broadly commercial context that the law recognizes as having a value by _____.

2. These two characteristics are _____ for understanding the _____ for protecting intellectual property rights.

3. Patent is a _____ right granted by the Government through the Patents Office to an individual who has invented _____.

4. Copyright is an _____ right to deal with _____ literary, dramatic, artistic and musical works.

5. The right of confidential information is something that is available to _____ the use of _____ and other confidential information without the owner's authority.

B. You are going to hear the statement the second time. Answer questions after listening.

1. What are the common characteristics of intellectual property?

   _____

   _____

123

2. What are the basic objectives for granting patent?

_____

_____

3. On what aspects are the rights in the trademark based on common law?

_____

_____

What Are the Types of Infringement of Intellectual Property?

You are going to hear the statement about the introduction of infringement of intellectual property. Have a dictation of the description. You will hear the recording three times.

_____

_____

_____

_____

_____

Part IV　Watching and Speaking

Basic Facts— Trademarks, Patents, and Copyrights

Watch the video and then discuss with your partner about your understanding of the basic facts about trademarks, patents, and copyrights, and share your opinion with the class.

**Lesson 20
Protection of Intellectual Property**

New IP Threat to Foreign Companies in China

Watch the video and then discuss with your partner about your understanding of new IP threat to foreign companies in China, and share your opinion with the class.

Part V Research and Presentation

Divide into groups, and try to interview some people about the following questions. Note down their answers and then make a presentation in class to introduce your findings.

1. What is intellectual property?

2. What are the rights given to the copyright holder?

3. Does the patent protection have a finite term?

4. What are the functions of trademarks?

5. How can you acquire a trademark?

6. List three important provisions used to regulate intellectual property.

_____

_____

Part VI Case Study

Debbie Elliott and *New York Times Magazine* ethicist Randy Cohen examine the dilemma that search engine Google poses with its Google Book Search tool. The powerful software can scan the whole sections of books for reading online.

Does Google's way cause copyright infringement?

Lesson 21

UNITED NATIONS CONVENTION ON CONTRACTS FOR THE INTERNATIONAL SALE OF GOODS

Part I Getting Ready

The following words and phrases will appear in this unit. Use five minutes to find out the meanings of these words and phrases.

Listen carefully and study them.

1. Offer
2. Invitation for offer
3. Withdraw and revocation of an offer
4. Acceptance
5. Counteroffer
6. Remedies
7. Fundamental breach of the contract
8. Anticipatory breach
9. Preservation of the goods
10. CISG
11. Subject matter
12. Bills of Exchange
13. International Promissory Notes

14. Take priority
15. International conventions

Part II Overview

A. Try to determine invitation for offer, offer and acceptance in the cases of going shopping, taking taxi and auction.

Case 1: Going shopping: the goods are placed on the shelves; the customer picks up the desired goods; the customer makes payment.

Case 2: Taking taxi: Opinion 1: the taxi is vacant or available; the passenger waves his hand to the taxi. Opinion 2: the taxi is vacant; waving to the taxi; boarding the taxi.

Case 3: Auction: public announcement; making bid by potential buyers; fall of hammer.

B. Do you know what the obligations of the seller and the buyer are? Exchange your opinion with your partner.

Part III Listening and Speaking

A. You are going to hear the statement about the formation of the contract. Fill in the blanks with the words you have heard in the following sentences after the first listening.

1. A proposal_____ to specific persons indicating an intention by the offeror _____ to the sale or purchase of particular goods for a price.

Lesson 21
United Nations Convention on Contracts for the International Sale of Goods

2. Proposals made to the public are _____ to negotiate, unless the _____ is clearly indicated.
3. Offers that do not state that they are _____ can be revoked any time before the offeree _____ an acceptance.
4. In accordance with the CISG rule, an offeror's _____ to keep an offer open for a fixed period is _____ .
5. Acceptance is a _____ or conduct by the offeree indicating _____ that is communicated to the offeror.

B. You are going to hear the statement the second time, and answer questions after listening.

1. What does definiteness of proposal mean?
   _____
   _____

2. When does the offer become effective?
   _____
   _____

3. When does the contract come into existence?
   _____
   _____

Transactions Covered in CISG

You are going to hear the statement about transactions covered in CISG. Have a dictation of the description. You will hear the recording three times.

_____
_____
_____
_____

129

Part IV Watching and Speaking

Revoking Your Offer or Counter Offer

Watch the video and then discuss with your partner about your understanding of revoking your offer or counter offer, share your opinion with the class.

What Are Some Remedies for Breach of Contract?

Watch the video and then discuss with your partner about remedies for breach of contract. Share your opinion with the class.

Part V Research and Presentation

Divide into groups, and try to interview some people about the following questions. Note down their answers and then make a presentation in class to introduce your findings.

1. Does silence constitute acceptance?

   _____
   _____

2. What is international sale of goods? What are the essential elements in an international sale of goods?

   _____
   _____

Lesson 21
United Nations Convention on Contracts for the International Sale of Goods

3. What are the differences between withdrawal of an offer and revocation of an offer?

___

4. How do you understand Mirror Image Rule?

___

5. What is fundamental breach? What is avoidance and can you explain the requirements for it?

___

6. List some laws which may affect a contract for the international sale of goods.

___

Part VI   Case Study

Asante, a Delaware corporation with its headquarters in California, ordered component parts for the switchers it manufactures from PMC-Sierra, a Delaware corporation with headquarters in British Columbia. Four of the five orders were placed through Unique Tech., one of PMC-Sierra's authorized distributors in California, but the fifth was sent by fax directly to PMC-Sierra in BC. Asante sued PMC-Sierra in a California court. PMC-Sierra had the suit removed to a US federal court. Asante now challenges the removal. (Note: Both the US and Canada are parties to the CISG.)

1. Does federal jurisdiction attach to claims governed by CISG?

___

2. Were the parties from two different CISG states?

3. Did the parties' choice of law clause exclude the CISG?

4. Does the well-pleaded complaint rule prevent the assumption of federal jurisdiction?

Lesson 22
ECONOMIC LAW AND TYPES OF PROPERTY

Part I Getting Ready

The following words and phrases will appear in this unit. Use five minutes to find out the meanings of these words and phrases.

Listen carefully and study them.

1. Economic law
2. Law and Economics
3. Personal property
4. Real property
5. Be attached to
6. Tangible
7. Intangible
8. Intellectual property
9. Chattels
10. Deed
11. Instruments of conveyance
12. Execute
13. Notarize
14. Quitclaim

Part II Overview

A. You are going to hear the statement about the definition of economic law. Fill in the blanks with the words you have heard in the following sentences after listening.

1. In the legal system of the _____ , economic law was the legal _____ and _____ under which economic relations were a legal discipline independent of _____ and _____ .

2. The economic law will _____ crucial economic relations and their _____ that often become the agreed _____ for national regulation across economic _____ .

3. Economic concepts are used to explain the _____ of laws, to assess which legal rules are economically _____ , and to predict which legal rules will be _____ .

B. You are going to hear the statement the second time, and answer questions after listening.

1. Do all the countries have economic law?
   _____
   _____

2. If they don't, for instance, in the United States, what is the corresponding law to economic law?
   _____
   _____

3. What is the purpose of economic law?
   _____
   _____

Lesson 22
Economic Law and Types of Property

4. Scholars from the University of Chicago introduced terminologies as Law and Economics or Economic Analysis of Law, what are their applications?

_____

_____

Part III Further Understanding

The Property Law

A. Now you have heard the types and elaboration of property in legal terms, please fill in the chart after listening to the statement.

Chart I

Types	Features (use "√" and "×" to mark the features)
P_____ property	Movable ( ) Subject to ownership ( ) Attached to land ( ) Chattels ( )
R_____ property	Movable ( ) Subject to ownership ( ) Attached to land ( ) Chattels ( )

Chart II Fill in the blanks and choose the numbers of correspondent items.

Tangible item ( )	Can be _____ or _____	1. Office furniture 2. Stocks 3. Business goods 4. Bonds
Intangible item ( )	Cannot be _____ or _____	5. Intellectual property 6. Business equipment 7. Money 8. Business vehicles

B. Choose the right one according to the statement or question.

1. Real property includes all items that would normally remain in place when an owner of real property moves. These items are known as _____.

    A. furniture

    B. fixtures

    C. fittings

    D. furnishings

    E. fixings

2. Which of the followings is NOT an example of personal property?

    A. Jewelry.

    B. Furniture.

    C. Stock certificates.

    D. Garage.

3. Which of the followings is NOT an example of real property?

    A. Garden.

    B. Swing set.

    C. Mailbox.

    D. Couch.

Lesson 22
Economic Law and Types of Property

Part IV Watching and Speaking

A. Fill in the blanks.

Now, you're a real estate attorney! Mary Mulligan and her three sisters are selling their family home. It's been in their family for almost a century and changed hands within their family many times. They've hired you to help them because this will be the first time it will be owned by someone outside of the Mulligan family, and there's a lot involved to make sure this conveyance, or property transfer, goes smoothly. Try to do your work as a professional, and you may need to:

1. start by discussing the _____ with Mary and her sisters.

2. introduce the definition of _____, which is _____
   _____.

3. sell the family home to Max, and complete the draft so that it meets particular execution, or procedural requirements:

   Identify the _____

   Identify the _____

   Identify the _____ using the legal description

   Be signed by the person _____ the property and

   That signature must be properly _____.

4. find out the survey of the family home, if it's not done, or that one was done but it's been lost. You'll need to _____ this issue. If there's no recent legal _____ of this property, then you'll need to _____ a survey of this property so that an accurate legal _____ can be added to the new deed.

5. decide which type of deeds shall be used in this scenario for the sake of Mary and her sisters, either _____ or _____.

B. Write down what you have heard.

_____
_____
_____
_____
_____

Part V   Speaking Task

A. Please use your own words to explain what economic law is briefly.

B. You and your partner are now supposed to have a conversation. In this conversation, each of you will give five examples of personal property and real property.

Lesson 23
LAWS AND ACTS OF SECURITY

Part I Getting Ready

The following words and phrases will appear in this unit. Use five minutes to find out the meanings of these words and phrases.

Listen carefully and study them.

1. Security
2. Constitution
3. Stocks
4. Shares
5. Bonds
6. Solicitation
7. Disclosure
8. Exemption
9. Proxy
10. Insider Trading
11. Registration
12. Insurance

法律英语视听说
Legal English Video-Aural-Oral Course

Part II Overview

A. You are going to hear the news report from Xinhua Press on Japanese government sued over constitutionality of security laws. Please listen carefully, and choose one right answer according to the question.

1. What is the report mainly about?

   A. Japanese class-action lawsuits of government safeguard to their citizens.

   B. Some Japanese sued the National Security Secretariat for not having fulfilled the job.

   C. Japanese class-action lawsuits of the constitutionality of the new security laws.

   D. Some Japanese sued the Democratic Party for military misconduct.

2. In this report, which article of Japan's Constitution is mentioned, stating that Japan will forever renounce war and will not maintain armed forces, or use force as a means of settling international disputes?

   A. Article 9.   B. Article 70.

   C. Article 15.   D. Article 19.

3. Which city is NOT mentioned in this report?

   A. Tokyo.   B. Hiroshima.

   C. Nagasaki.   D. Hokkaido.

4. What is the attitude of Japan's government?

   A. Saying the security laws are unconstitutional.

   B. Saying the security laws are constitutional.

   C. None of the government department has responded yet.

   D. The report didn't say.

5. What is the meaning of the word "security" in this report?

   A. The state of being free from danger or injury.

   B. An electrical device that sets off an alarm when someone tries to break in.

Lesson 23
Laws and Acts of Security

C. A guarantee that an obligation will be met.

D. Stocks, shares, bonds, or other certificates that you buy in order to earn regular interest from them or to sell them later for a profit.

B. Fill in the blanks.

1. For the past 70 years since the end of _____, Japan's pacifist constitution has effectively _____ the peace and security of its citizens by _____ its own war potential.

2. The _____ maintain that Japanese forces _____ the right to collective self-defense is in _____ of Japan's Supreme Law and could cause the nation "_____."

Part III Further Understanding

Securities Act of 1933

A. Now please answer the following questions and complete the chart.

1. What does *Securities Act of 1933* often refer to?

   _____

   _____

2. What are the basic two objectives of *Securities Act of 1933*?

   _____

   _____

3. What information will be registered in the US regarding security?

   _____

   _____

4. What is the full name of SRO?
   _____
   _____

5. Followed by *Securities Act of 1933*, *Securities Exchange Act of 1934* empowers the SEC with broad authority over all aspects of the securities industry, name some of the powers.
   _____
   _____

B. Listen to the passage again, and finish the following chart.

Securities Act of 1933

Require _____

Prohibit _____

Exemptions from the registration requirement:
1. Private _____ to a limited number of persons or institutions;
2. Offerings of _____ size;
3. _____ offerings;
4. Securities of _____, state, and federal governments.

Securities Exchange Act of 1934

SEC, which is: _____

Companies with more than $ ____ million in assets whose securities are held by more than ____ owners must file annual and other periodic reports.

Proxy Solicitations: disclosure in materials used to ____ shareholders' votes in ____ or special meetings.

Tender Offers: information by anyone seeking to acquire more than ____ percent of a company's securities by direct purchase or tender offer.

Insider Trading: a person trades a ____ while in possession of ____ nonpublic information in ____ of a duty to withhold the information or refrain from trading.

Registration of Exchanges, Associations, and Others: the Act requires a variety of market participants to register with the Commission, including ____, ____ and dealers, ____ agents, and ____ agencies.

Lesson 23
Laws and Acts of Security

Rule 504 of Securities

A. Click the ones which are exempt securities.

☐ Government securities

☐ Bonds

☐ Foreign government securities

☐ Bank or financial institution securities

☐ Money markets

☐ CDs

☐ Insurance

☐ Public utility and railroad securities

☐ Non-profit securities

☐ Employee benefit plans

B. Choose the right answers according to the statement.

Rule 504 allows a company to sell securities if one of the following conditions is met:

A. The company must register the offering exclusively in a state where registration is required, and financial disclosure must be provided to investors.

B. The company sells in both a state that requires registration and in one that does not require registration and provide full financial disclosure.

C. The company sells to accredited investors in a state that permits general solicitation and advertising.

D. An exempt security is advertised to a particular state's residents, there may be a law about registration.

E. Exempt securities can only be sold to accredited investors.

Part IV Speaking Task

So you are now a speaker, your topic today is to tell people what insider trading is and what penalties people will be charged once they have engaged in insider trading. Try to make your speech organized and use the information you've heard in the previous passage.

Lesson 24

BUSINESS LAW: CONSUMER PROTECTION AND PRODUCT LIABILITY

Part I Getting Ready

The following words and phrases will appear in this unit. Use five minutes to find out the meanings of these words and phrases.

Listen carefully and study them.

1. Consumer protection
2. Product liability
3. Federal Trade Commission
4. Consumerism
5. Unscrupulous
6. Beyond a reasonable doubt
7. Credulous
8. Misrepresentations
9. Wrongdoing
10. Subsidiaries

Part II Overview

What Is Consumer Protection?

Listen to the following introduction, and answer the questions.

1. What do you think consumerism refers to, as in "America is known for its consumerism"?

2. What is the focus of the Federal Trade Commission (FTC)?

3. What rights does FTC protect?

4. What legal doctrine helps with consumer protection?

5. Are product liability laws state laws or federal laws?

6. Write down three main types of product liability.

Lesson 24
Business Law: Consumer Protection and Product Liability

Part III Further Understanding

Consumer Protection Legislation in EU

A. Choose the right answer.

1. Which is NOT relevant to EU's consumer protection legislation? Please make a mark.

   ☐ The Charter of Fundamental Rights

   ☐ The Directive on Consumer Rights

   ☐ The Federal Trade Commission

   ☐ The guidance document

2. When is the time for the adoption of the Directive according to the passage?

   A. 2011.   B. 1999.

   C. 2017.   D. 2014.

3. Which might NOT be the subject of consumer protection?

   A. Food and product safety.   B. Data protection.

   C. Supermarket purchase.   D. National security protection.

4. What example does the passage illustrate about vulnerable consumer?

   A. Person with disabilities.   B. The elder.

   C. The adolescence.   D. The less affluent.

5. What is "notion that the asymmetry of information"?

   A. The seller should sell perfect product.

   B. The seller should not set the price too high.

   C. The seller should be deemed to know more than the buyer.

   D. The seller should guarantee the after service to consumers.

B. Write down what you have heard.

_____
_____
_____
_____
_____
_____
_____
_____

Unfair or Deceptive Trade Practices

A. Listen to the passage carefully and complete the following chart.

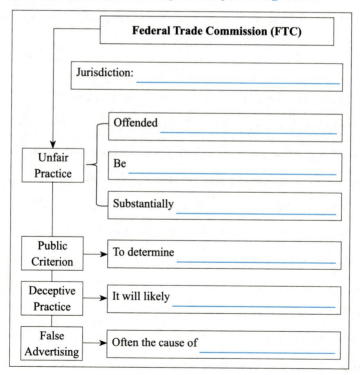

Lesson 24
Business Law: Consumer Protection and Product Liability

B. Fill in the blanks with proper words.

| A. federal | B. statutes | C. substantial | D. credulous |
| E. beyond a reasonable doubt | F. prosecutor | G. misrepresentations | |

1. The Federal Trade Commission (FTC), the largest _____ agency.
2. _____ consumers are prone to believe any advertisement.
3. The FTC can issue a cease and desist order, compelling the advertiser to make corrections or disclosures informing the public of the _____.
4. In addition, every state has enacted consumer protection _____.
5. In criminal law, _____ is a very important notion.
6. Tom works as a _____, and he fights against criminal suspect.
7. _____ injury of consumers is the most heavily weighed element.

Part IV Speaking Task

A. You are supposed to conclude the main idea of this passage as a lawyer. State clearly about the three types of defects.

B. Please use your own words to connect the consumer protection and product liability in the US.

Lesson 25
LAW OF CONTRACT(1): BASIC PRINCIPLES

Part I Getting Ready

The following words and phrases will appear in this unit. Use five minutes to find out the meanings of these words and phrases.

Listen carefully and study them.

1. Binding
2. Duration
3. Labour protection
4. Offer
5. Acceptance
6. Consideration
7. Minor
8. Capacity
9. Mutual assent
10. Enforceable

Lesson 25
Law of Contract(1): Basic Principles

Part II Overview

A. Please listen to the conversation and choose the right words and phrases to complete the sentences. And please use simple expressions to conclude what the woman should do before her signing up the contract.

| A. binding | B. payment | C. duration | D. sick leave |
| E. labour protection | F. bonus | G. flawless | H. occupational safety |
| I. lest |

1. Contract is a legally _____ agreement.
2. That contract he drafted is really _____.
3. What attached my attention is the extremely fat _____ in that company.
4. The _____ of that agreement is from June 1st last year to May 30th next year.
5. The company carries out many dangerous tasks in the mountain area. It shall establish and prefect the system for _____ and health, working standard and production process.
6. Have you made it clear that you want the _____ monthly?
7. I got a cold last week, so I could just ask for a _____.
8. It's just incredible that the climbing club has provide such considerable _____ to their coaches.
9. Don't approach the cliff, _____ you fall down.

B. What should the woman do before her signing up the contract?

_____
_____
_____

151

Part III Further Understanding

Basic Principles of the Law of Contract

A. Listen to this passage, and try to answer the following questions. Please write down the information in the following chart according to the passage.

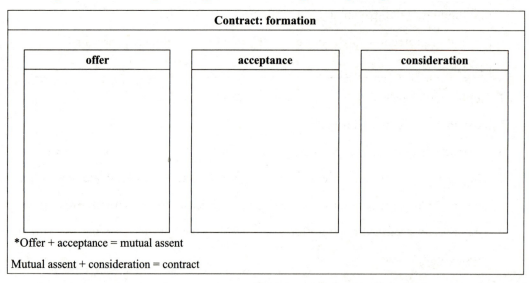

B. Now, listen to the passage for the second time, and answer the questions according to what you've heard.

1. What does the law of contract state?

   _____
   _____

2. In the example of purchasing the underlying property, what are the features of the offer?

   _____
   _____

Lesson 25
Law of Contract(1): Basic Principles

3. What should be followed after the offer?

　

4. When the offered party proposes a counteroffer, what should they do?

　

5. For what purposes will the basic principles of the law of contract require consideration to be given?

　

6. Name some forms of consideration.

　

Capacity in Contract Law—Minor

A. Please fill in the blanks with the words you have heard in the following sentences.

1. There are groups who have limitations when entering into a contract, for example, the _____ , _____ party, and _____ party.
2. Those individuals who are under the age of 18 are recognised as _____ .
3. Contracts that are considered for the benefit of the minor are that of _____ , education, _____ , _____ and employment.
4. If a contract is _____ and money is paid by a minor, then usually it cannot be recovered unless it can be proved that the contract has not been _____ to the minor.
5. A court would never _____ someone — whether that person is an adult or a minor — to perform a contract for _____ due to a matter of

_____ that parties should not be _____ to continue in a personal relationship against their _____.

B. Please answer the following questions based on the passage you've heard.

1. If a boy aged 14 entered a contract to a club for singing and dancing, and the contract had conditions which were considered not beneficial to him, is the boy bound by the contract?

   _____
   _____

2. Related to the previous question, explain the answer you have provided.

   _____
   _____

Part IV Speaking Task

This passage mainly discusses the capacity in contract law concerning ages of the party. Do you think there will be other factors in capacity in contract law? Discuss with your partner, and make your own conclusion.

Lesson 25
Law of Contract(1): Basic Principles

Part V Case Study

A. Now imagine you are a counsel for your client. Listen to this passage and then try to introduce the following concepts to your client.

1. When asked by your client how a contract can be enforceable, you may tell them: It must contain:

   A. an offer that _____

   B. acceptance, which is _____

   C. consideration, _____

   D. capacity of the parties in terms of _____

   E. the intent of both parties to _____

   F. legally enforceable terms and conditions, also called _____

2. Now Josie Aurora decided to rent an apartment from your client Landlord Whistler, the Landlord may need to

   A. sign _____ ;

   B. charge the _____ to secure the apartment;

   C. hand over the _____ to Josie afterwards.

   The process of formation of lease in this way is called to enter into an _____ contract.

B. As for an implied in-fact contract, it binds parties together through a mutual agreement and intent, but there are no expressed terms of the agreement. List three elements in the passage.

_____

_____

_____

_____

Lesson 26

LAW OF CONTRACT (2): BREACH AND REMEDIES

Part I Getting Ready

The following words and phrases will appear in this unit. Use five minutes to find out the meanings of these words and phrases.

Listen carefully and study them.

1. Breach
2. Material
3. Equity law
4. Negligent
5. Substantial
6. Compensate
7. Remedies
8. Damages
9. Mutuality

Lesson 26
Law of Contract (2): Breach and Remedies

Part II Overview

Definition: Breach of Contract

A. Write down the key information when you are listening for the first time.

B. And now, please supply the missing information on the brief card of the term "breach of contract."

Breach of Contract	
Legal sense:	_____ to fulfill contractual obligations
Categories:	_____ and _____
Aspect: (civil law or criminal law?)	_____
Legal solution:	_____
Common law:	_____
Equity law:	_____

C. Also, you need to supply the missing information in the next chart in order to make a clearer look of how to determine materiality.

Factors that the courts consider in determining materiality
1. The amount of _____ ;
2. Whether the non-breaching party _____ ;
3. The _____ of performance by the breaching party;
4. _____ to the breaching party;
5. _____ or _____ behavior of the breaching party; and
6. The _____ that the breaching party will perform the _____ of the contract.

D. Now listen to the passage for the second time, and with the help of the charts, arrange the following items.

1. Failure to fulfill any of its contractual obligations.

2. Entering into a contract.

3. Resort to remedies.

4. Having the immediate right to all remedies.

5. Proving the materiality of the breaching party.

The correct order should be:

_____

E. Please decide whether the breach is material or not, write "T" when it is, write "F" when it's not.

[ ] 1. If the contract specifies the sale of a box of tennis balls and the buyer receives a box of footballs.

[ ] 2. If the contract specifies the sale of a box of tennis balls and the buyer receives a box of tennis balls with one of them broken.

Lesson 26
Law of Contract (2): Breach and Remedies

[ ] 3. If a homeowner and an electrician agreed to have the electrician wire the home using a type of yellow wire but the electrician ended up using blue wire.

[ ] 4. If a homeowner and an electrician agreed to have the electrician wire the home using a type of copper wire but the electrician ended up using aluminum wire.

[ ] 5. If the buyer and the seller agreed the deal of ten cupcakes of strawberry flavor, but the seller sent ten blueberry flavor cupcakes to the buyer.

Breach of Contract

A. Please fill in the blanks in the following sentences.

1. Contracts are usually made in an effort to _____ an agreement and to protect the parties in the agreement.

2. A remedy is when a court enforces a right or satisfies a legal harm or injury through _____ .

3. A partial breach is also sometimes referred to as an _____ breach.

4. Sometimes a party will fail to uphold a _____ portion of the contract. The breached portion is sometimes _____ to the rest of the contract, affecting the main _____ of the contract.

5. A material breach is usually _____ by excusing the _____ party from any further _____ under the contract.

B. Write down what you have heard.

_____
_____
_____
_____
_____
_____

Part III Case Study

Now, you have heard about a few ways in which a contract ends. If you are a lawyer, when you come across these situations, you may (click the answers which seem correct to you):

☐ 1. sue the painter for he has promised to complete the work by July 15, but failed to do so;

☐ 2. ignore his delay so long as he can finish in reasonable timeframe;

☐ 3. not believe the painter will finish his job because of his breach;

☐ 4. take his breach as a non-material breach;

☐ 5. take his breach as a material breach.

Part IV Speaking Task

When the painter promised to finish your deck while he has been absent from work for half a month, which will definitely lead to delay? You will talk to him right now, explain to him about the outcome of his breach. Try to do it on a legal basis.

Lesson 27

ANTITRUST LAW AND SHERMAN ACT

Part I Getting Ready

The following words and phrases will appear in this unit. Use five minutes to find out the meanings of these words and phrases.

Listen carefully and study them.

1. Antitrust
2. Abuses of a dominant position
3. Market share
4. Complacency
5. Monopoly
6. Market allocation
7. Bid rigging
8. Sherman Antitrust Act
9. Trust busting
10. Jointly managed companies

Part II Overview

News Interview

A. You are going to hear a CNN news interview in April, 2016. In the following part, they are discussing the case of Google in Europe. Listen carefully, and answer the following questions based on the interview.

1. What is the company involved in the case of this interview?

2. Does the European commission consider it has strong case against the company, and why?

3. According to a lot of critics, what is EU attempting to do?

4. Which company's case is mentioned to make the comparison?

5. According to the man, what will the European commission focus on for the case?

B. Which processes will the company go through, according to the interview? Click the possible ones.

☐ Respondent letter

Lesson 27
Antitrust Law and Sherman Act

☐ Hearing

☐ Defense actions

☐ Counterclaim

☐ Complaint

☐ Discrimination

☐ Settlement

C. Now listen to the interview again, and write a short report.

If you are a Chinese journalist, write a short report in this case based on this interview. State the ideas presented by both sides.

Part III Further Understanding

Antitrust Law

Complete the following chart.

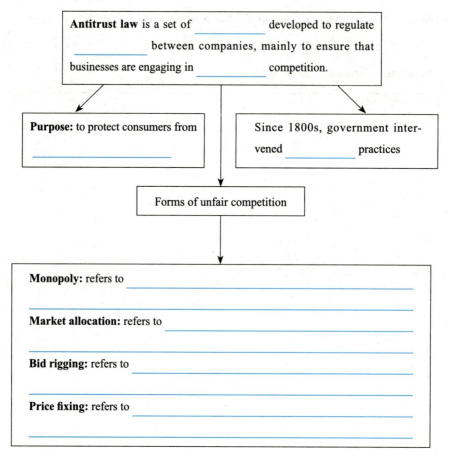

Antitrust law is a set of _____ developed to regulate _____ between companies, mainly to ensure that businesses are engaging in _____ competition.

Purpose: to protect consumers from _____

Since 1800s, government intervened _____ practices

Forms of unfair competition

Monopoly: refers to _____

Market allocation: refers to _____

Bid rigging: refers to _____

Price fixing: refers to _____

Lesson 27
Antitrust Law and Sherman Act

Trusts and Monopolies

A. Choose the right answer to each of the questions.

1. What does the Sherman Antitrust Act mainly focus on?

    A. It focuses on real estate.

    B. It focuses on constitution law.

    C. It focuses on trust and unfair competition.

    D. It focuses on economic data.

2. Which is the best substitute name of Sherman Antitrust Act?

    A. Interstate Commerce Law.

    B. Competition Law.

    C. Company Law.

    D. Monopoly Law.

3. Which is probably NOT the behavior of a trust?

    A. Dominating major industries.

    B. Destroying competition.

    C. Jointly management.

    D. Economic liberalism.

4. Which American President has actually pushed forward the process of the Sherman Act, and made a considerable success?

    A. President Roosevelt.

    B. President Taft.

    C. President Hayes.

    D. President Bush.

B. Write down what you have heard.

_____
_____
_____
_____
_____

Part IV Speaking Task

Based on the chart you've completed in accordance with Antitrust Law, use your own words to deliver an introduction of antitrust law.

Lesson 28
TYPES AND LAWS OF COMPETITION

Part I Getting Ready

The following words and phrases will appear in this unit. Use five minutes to find out the meanings of these words and phrases.

Listen carefully and study them.

1. Competition
2. Revenue
3. Empirical
4. Vacated
5. Unbundling
6. Mandate
7. Tort
8. Misappropriate
9. Manufacture
10. Deceptive

Part II Overview

What Is Competition?

A. According to the passage, competition motivates companies to increase sales volume by utilizing the four components of the marketing mix, also referred to as the four P's, which are:

P_____;

P_____;

P_____;

And, P_____.

B. Complete the missing information, and choose the correspondent definition.

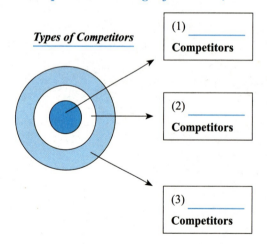

Types of Competitors

(1) _____ **Competitors** — Something that someone could do instead of choosing your product

(2) _____ **Competitors** — Offers the same products and services, but the end goals are different. These competitors are seeking to grow revenue with a different strategy.

(3) _____ **Competitors** — Offers the same products and services aimed at the same target market and customer base, with the same goal of profit and market-share growth.

**Lesson 28
Types and Laws of Competition**

C. Now, analyze what competition types connected to X-Space in the following case:
There is a game company named X-Space who is right now promoting a new on-line game of Gunfire; another game company C-Factor meanwhile is promoting their game of Wartime; the third company named Yetet is promoting a software which can help players speed up in game playing; and the forth company sells military books in the market.

_____
_____
_____
_____
_____

Part III   Case Study

Supreme Court of the United States

ON WRITS OF CERTIORARI TO THE UNITED STATES COURT OF APPEALS FOR THE EIGHTH CIRCUIT

Click the right ones according to the writs, then answer the questions.

1. Companies concerned in this judge's opinion:

   AT&T

   MCI

   Sprint.

   NYNEX

   Bell Atlantic

Among those, who is the party concerned in this case?
_____
_____

2. What is the issue in this case?
_____
_____

3. Why is it involved in the unfair competition?
_____
_____

4. Telecommunications Law and Policy 411—412 (2d ed. 1998) (explaining rationale of the decree) is mentioned in this judge's opinion, and how does it respond to this argument?

First, it creats _____,
and in setting forth the second alternative, the Act _____
_____

5. What is the judge's final standing point in this case?
_____
_____

Part IV Watching and Applying

Unfair Competition: *Welcome to Barks and Bubbles!*

A. Now you are the lawyer of the speaker, who wants to file a lawsuit against her ex-employee, Wilma. Based on the information you've heard, finish the following tasks.

1. What is an unfair competition?
_____
_____

Lesson 28
Types and Laws of Competition

2. What did Wilma do?

   [Logo] _____

   [Marketing list] _____

   [Trade secrets] _____

   [Advertisement] _____

   [Price] _____

3. Complete the following words and phrases under the category of "trade secrets" according to the given letter.

   A trade secret is any confidential business information that provides the business with a competitive edge. This includes things like s_____ methods, d_____ methods, m_____ methods, r_____ methods, c_____, ad_____, s_____ lists, c_____ lists, firm s_____, and m_____ processes.

B. Now, please write a legal letter to Wilma on behalf of your client.

+--+
| XYZ Law Firm |
| Date _____ |
| Wilma Smith, |
| 301# Queen Ave., New York |
| |
| _____ |
| _____ |
| _____ |
| _____ |
| _____ |
| _____ |
| _____ |
| _____ |
| _____ |
+--+

Lesson 29
CRIMINAL LAW (1): BASIC PRINCIPLES

Part I   Getting Ready

The following words and phrases will appear in this unit. Use five minutes to find out the meanings of these words and phrases.

Listen carefully and study them.

1. Exclusive
2. Cause of action
3. Burglary
4. Wrongdoer
5. Criminal justice system
6. Predator
7. Gang leader
8. Trial
9. Obstruction of justice
10. Discovery of evidence

Lesson 29
Criminal Law (1): Basic Principles

Part II Overview

Definitions and Differences

A. Choose the right answer to each of the questions.

1. Which of the followings is a legal remedy in a civil case?

    A. Jail. B. Prison. C. Damages.

    D. Criminal fine. E. Capital punishment.

2. What is NOT the type of criminal law?

    A. Burglary. B. Robbery. C. Assault.

    D. Arson. E. Torts.

3. Who will be the party and initiate the prosecution?

    A. The victim. B. The government. C. The police.

4. Why do we think criminal cases are considered to be wrongs committed against society as a whole?

    A. They put the community in fear.

    B. They undermine public confidence.

    C. They cause financial damages to people.

    D. They infringe the rights between parties.

B. Write down your own version of definition of cause of action according to what you've heard.

_____

_____

_____

C. Write down what you have heard.

_____
_____
_____
_____
_____

News Report

A. Listen to the passage and do the exercises.

1. What is the main idea that the President is calling for?

   _____
   _____

2. _____ and _____ are jailed for _____ drug crimes at much higher rates than other groups of people.

3. The president's _____ was part of his effort to _____ the criminal justice system. The 46 prisoners were in jail for crimes involving the _____. The _____ time in prison for such crimes is much _____ than for crimes related to regular cocaine.

B. Listen to this report again, and write down a short report accordingly. You are supposed to use no more than 150 words to retell the report.

_____
_____
_____
_____
_____

**Lesson 29
Criminal Law (1): Basic Principles**

Settlement

In this section, there is some background information about settlement. Use three minutes to finish reading them, then you will watch a clip of a legal TV show. Watch carefully, and answer the questions below.

A settlement, as well as dealing with the dispute between the parties is a contract between those parties.

Generally, when a settlement is reached in the U.S., it will be submitted to the court to be "rolled into a court order." This is done so that the court which was initially assigned the case may retain jurisdiction over it. The court is then free to modify its order as necessary to achieve justice in the case, and a party that breaches the settlement may be held in contempt of court, rather than facing only a civil claim for the breach.

During a negotiation, it is very important to express your standpoint clearly and to handle the whole negotiation. Let us look at the useful expressions in negotiation.

Here are some useful sentences concerning negotiation.
1. "The offer is 40 thousand, good for 1 week."
2. "Take it or leave it!"
3. "This proposal is non-negotiable."
4. "Don't ask me to go back to my client on this. This is all we are going to do."
5. "This is it. If you don't want to accept it at that price, forget it."

Choose the following words to fill in the blanks in each sentence. Please remember to change the form of the verbs if necessary.

contempt	breach	enforce	drop	retain
liability	initiate	intervention		

1. If there is a civil case in your jurisdiction and the parties reach a settlement before trial, then the suit will be _____ .

2. Meanwhile, the jurisdiction over the original case will be _____.
3. After the settlement is reached, the court will _____ the settlement.
4. If the settlement is _____, the non-breach party _____ a civil cause of action in connection with the breach or seek _____ by the court.
5. And you, as the judge of the court, can decide the breach party both the _____ of breach and _____ of the court.

Part III Speaking Task

Now you will watch three clips of different criminal trials in different countries. Please discuss with your partner, and do the following tasks.

1. Discuss the major differences you noticed in the three videos.
2. Discuss the cultural backgrounds making those differences.
3. Share with your class about your personal understanding of criminal trial procedure's impact with different characteristics.

Lesson 30
CRIMINAL LAW(2): PLEA BARGAINING AND CROSS EXAMINATION

Part I Getting Ready

The following words and phrases will appear in this unit. Use five minutes to find out the meanings of these words and phrases.

Listen carefully and study them.

1. Plea bargaining
2. Suspended sentence
3. Pending
4. Fine
5. Discretion
6. Arraignment
7. Misdemeanor
8. Provoke
9. Badgering the witness
10. Testify

Part II Overview

Arraignment

Finish the following questions based on the passage.

1. Where does this statement take place?

   _____
   _____

2. What is the purpose of this statement?

   _____
   _____

3. What will happen if you plea guilty?

   _____
   _____

4. You have the rights to remain _____ and not have that fact _____ by the judge or _____ at trial. To an _____ and right to have an _____ appointed if you cannot afford one if the court is considering a _____ on this charge.

5. To _____ at trial and have your testimony considered by the standard as the other _____. To have a reporter make a complete record of _____. To _____ any harmful _____ to a higher court.

Lesson 30
Criminal Law(2): Plea Bargaining and Cross Examination

Opening Statement

Answer the following questions.

1. Who is giving this opening statement?

   _____
   _____

2. When you have been charged with a misdemeanor, what will you face?

   _____
   _____

3. If you enter a plea of not guilty, will you be set for trial?

   _____
   _____

4. If you violated a county ordinance and not a very serious one, will you plea guilty, and why?

   _____
   _____

5. Can you hire your own lawyer to represent you at the beginning of the case?

   _____
   _____

About the Plea Bargaining

Decide whether the following statements are true or false.

[ ] 1. It is a striking fact that trials are not the usual way that a defendant's fate is decided.

[ ] 2. Most prisoners behind bars did not get a chance to have a jury trial because they pleaded guilty.

[ ] 3. In the US, up to 90 percent of all convictions come about by plea bargaining.

[ ] 4. Plea bargaining is a compromise: both sides give a little, gain a little.

[   ] 5. Only a few criminal prosecutions are resolved by a guilty plea entered prior to trial, which serves as a waiver of the right to a trial.

Part III   Thinking and Speaking

Discuss the following questions.

1. Do you think plea bargaining is a reasonable scheme?
2. What is the difference between the plea bargaining in the US and the self-confession system in China?
3. To what extent do you think that the plea bargaining system could be introduced to China?

Part IV   Negotiations

Before listening to the material, use your background knowledge to decide whether the following statements are true or false.

[   ] 1. Cross-examination is preceded by direct examination.

[   ] 2. Leading question is only allowed during cross-examination.

[   ] 3. The attorney may ask the witness any kind of question related to the cases during the cross-examination.

[   ] 4. If a witness gives a testimony that is inconsistent with what the opposing party wants to lead as evidence, the opposing party must raise the contention with that witness during cross-examination.

Lesson 30
Criminal Law(2): Plea Bargaining and Cross Examination

Boston Legal

Watch the clip of a movie, think about the leading questions raised by the lawyer, and answer the following questions.

1. Why did the securities laugh and the judge seem confused during the cross-examination?

   _____
   _____

2. Why did the attorney ask about the windows and the trees? Isn't that obvious?

   _____
   _____

3. What useful information did the attorney obtain at last?

   _____
   _____

4. List some functions you would think of about cross-examination.

   _____
   _____

Badgering the Witness

Listen to the dialogue, and answer the questions.

1. Make a definition of "badgering the witness" based on what you've heard in this court examination.

   _____
   _____

2. If you are a lawyer, when your client is provoked in the witness seat during a trial, what can you do?

   _____
   _____

3. When the judge said she would hold the woman for contempt, what did the woman do?
_____
_____

4. Share with your partner about your understanding and advice from this dialogue.
_____
_____

Answers

Lesson 1 History of American Law
Part II
Exercise A

1. When we want to define a legal term, we can look to *Black's Law Dictionary*.

2. *Black's Law Dictionary* has been published since 1891.

3. *Black's Law Dictionary* defines law as "that which is laid down, ordained, or established..."

Exercise B

1. F

2. T

3. F

Exercise C

(1) murder

(2) stealing

(3) cheating on taxes

(4) society's morality

(5) business law

Exercise D

1. In America, our law system came from the Great Britain.

2. The English common law is rooted in centuries of English history.

3. Yes, it is.

Exercise E

1. Shortly before the American Revolution in the last half of the 18th century.

2. This publication spanned four volumes.

3. Judicial decisions are decisions made by a court and are also known as case law.

4. Because Founding Fathers were looking to establish a government, and they had no other viable reference to written law.

Part III

Exercise A

(1) common law

(2) settling disputes

(3) increasingly formalized

(4) together and organized

(5) basic principles

Exercise B

1. F

2. T

1. D

2. B

Exercise C

(1) previous cases

(2) current legal structure

(3) exists exactly

(4) ever-changing

(5) adoption

Exercise D

1. F

2. F

3. T

4. F

5. T

Answers

Exercise E

(1) Principles

(2) unwritten

(3) thorough compilation

(4) shape our American law system

(5) federal entities

(6) interpret new laws

Part IV

1. Before Luther Graves became a lawyer, he was a prosecutor.

2. D. A.s forget that getting the wrong person convicted is not a win. It is the worst loss in the world. So we have juries to remind them.

Lesson 2 Fundamental Doctrine: Stare Decisis Doctrine

Part II

Exercise A

(1) principle

(2) broken

(3) courts

(4) guide

(5) decision

(6) authority

(7) obligates

(8) case-by-case

Exercise B

(1) borrower

(2) borrowee

(3) permission

(4) breaks

(5) demands

(6) owe

(7) fix

(8) jurisdiction

Exercise C

1. F

2. F

3. T

4. T

Exercise D

1. A woman's right to abortion.

2. To protect the mother's health or the fetus' life.

3. The civil rights movement.

4. When the former precedent can no longer be justified, or it no longer reflects the majority views of the society.

Part III

Exercise A

1. F

2. T

3. F

4. T

Exercise B

(1) same-sex marriage

(2) a federal and a state law

(3) Defense

(4) violated

(5) the same tax, health and retirement benefits

(6) continue efforts to limit

Answers

Part IV

Exercise A

1. No, he contradicted the testimony.

2. He only possesses right hand.

3. Poor and ignorant.

4. She tempted a Negro.

5. Not guilty.

Exercise B

1. B

2. B

3. C

4. B

Lesson 3 Sources of Law (1)

Part II

Exercise A

1. C

2. A

3. B

The Congress	legislative branch
The president	judicial branch
The Supreme Court	executive branch.

(Congress — legislative branch; The president — executive branch; The Supreme Court — judicial branch)

Exercise B

(1) topics

(2) Interpretation

(3) entities

(4) branches

(5) nations

187

Exercise C

1. T

2. T

3. F

Exercise D

1. Congress is made up of the House of Representatives and the Senate.

2. Article II establishes the executive branch, which is the U. S. President.

3. Article IV.

4. The Bill of Rights.

5. Article VI.

Part III

Exercise A

1. Congress

2. houses

3. delegates

4. population

5. Senate

Exercise B

(1) president

(2) advisors

(3) executive

(4) carrying

(5) budget

(6) pardons

(7) national

(8) terms

Exercise C

1. F

Answers

2. T

3. F

4. T

5. F

Part IV

1. "Long time" and "Associate."

2. With the justification of "not in evidence."

Lesson 4 Sources of Law (2)

Part II

Exercise A

1. T

2. F

3. F

4. F

Exercise B

(1) powerful

(2) expands

(3) Constitution

(4) elastic

(5) execution

(6) additionally

(7) crimes

(8) enumerated

Exercise C

1. D

2. A

3. C

Exercise D

1. Regulatory law.

2. It covers many different types of issues, legal procedures, and regulations.

3. Generally speaking, there are two types of administrative law. The first type includes rules and regulations. The second type of administrative law includes administrative decisions.

4. Congress and state legislatures.

5. Government agencies.

Exercise E

1. F

2. T

3. F

4. F

1. Equal protection guarantees of general rights.

2. Business activity.

Exercise F

1. E

2. A

Part III

Exercise A

1. T

2. T

3. F

4. F

Answers

Lesson 5 Comparison of Laws

Part II

Exercise A

1. beadc

2. dbcea

Exercise B

(1) administrative

(2) demonstrates

(3) violated

(4) succession

(5) plaintiff

(6) compensation

(7) suffering

Part III

Exercise A

(1) Criminal and civil laws are not mutually exclusive; both can be used for a single event.

(2) The government must prove its case beyond a reasonable doubt.

(3) If the defendant is convicted, or found guilty, he or she will receive a punishment.

(4) This type of law deals with private rights and remedies by governing disputes between individuals, groups, and organizations.

(5) If the defendant is found liable, the plaintiff will likely receive a judgment for damages, which is money awarded to compensate for a loss or injury.

Exercise B

1. F

2. T

3. T

4. F

5. T

Exercise C

(1) E

(2) B

(3) A

(4) C

(5) D

Exercise D

1. Procedural law adheres to due process, which is a right granted to U. S. citizens by the 14th Amendment.

2. Due process refers to the legal rights owed to a person in criminal and civil actions. It is one of our 14th Amendment rights and guarantees the right to life, liberty and the pursuit of happiness.

3. He has rights to a speedy, fair and impartial trial.

Exercise E

1. C

2. B

3. C

Lesson 6 Types of Legal Actions

Part II

Exercise A

(1) trial court

(2) jurisdiction

(3) subject matter

(4) judgement

(5) claims

Exercise B

1.　　(3)　　(1)　　(5)　　(4)　　(6)　　(2)

Answers

2. (2) (5) (3) (6) (1) (4)

Exercise C

1. T
2. F
3. T
4. T

Part III

Exercise A

1. Civil actions must arise out of a violation of one's constitutional rights, a violation of law or treaties of the United States or if the United States is party to the suit.
2. A jury (or a judge).
1. 13.
2. Because this court hears appeals from the lower court, the judges' decisions often set legal precedent.

Exercise B

(1) Each level of court serves a different legal function for both civil and criminal cases.

(2) In this court, civil actions must arise out of a violation of one's constitutional rights.

(3) Criminal cases arise only when the United States is party to the suit.

(4) U. S. Circuit Court of Appeals resides over cases in where one or both parties are dissatisfied with the judgment in the U. S. District Court.

(5) U. S. Supreme Court is the highest court in a state (or in the United States) and generally only deals with matters of state or national importance or appeals from appellate court.

Exercise C

(1) B
(2) E
(3) A
(4) C

(5) D

Exercise D

1. B

2. B

3. C

Part IV

1. They serve a lifetime term with the exception of retirement, resignation or impeachment.

2. The losing party must file a writ of certiorari, or a request for permission to review the case.

3. The decision is final only when four of the nine justices vote to grant the writ.

Part V

Exercise A

1. Because the United States was a party to the suit.

2. The motion was granted to the plaintiff, the United States, making the defendant Hernandez liable to repay the monies borrowed with interest.

Exercise B

1. In the lower court, it was decided that the media was protected under First Amendment rights.

2. While no new evidence is brought to light in appellate court, a closer look at the application of law and constitutional rights are reviewed. And the lower court's decision was remanded and sent back for retrial.

Exercise C

1. Administration law.

2. Public law.

3. His conviction was rescinded.

4. The panel of justices overturned Arizona's state ruling citing that Miranda's constitutional rights had been violated.

Answers

Lesson 7 Legal Procedures

Part II

Exercise A

A plaintiff is a party who initiates a lawsuit or who yields allegations against another party.

A defendant is on the receiving end of the allegations.

A lawyer is a professional who represents a party in a court of law.

A judge is a professional who oversees and makes decisions in court cases.

Exercise B

A D E B C

Exercise C

(1) complaint

(2) cause of action

(3) summons

(4) answer

(5) default judgment

(6) counterclaim

(7) motion

(8) filed a lawsuit

(9) Information

(10) discovery

(11) Interrogatories

(12) Depositions

Part III

Exercise A

1. A complaint is a legal document that sets forth causes of action or claims of wrongdoing against both parties.

2. It will include names of parties, causes of action and where and when to appear in court.

3. The summons will contain information about the case and where and when to appear in court.

Exercise B

1. There may be a default judgment in favor of the plaintiff. This means the plaintiff wins by default.

2. Informal negotiations involve the parties sitting before a mediator to discuss options for settlement before a case ever reaches a courtroom.

3. The case would go to trial.

Part IV

Exercise A

1. F

2. F

3. T

4. F

Exercise B

1. T

2. F

3. T

4. F

Exercise C

The civil appeals process starts with a losing party in a civil trial. The losing party, or the appellant, files an appeal with a higher court, generally Federal court.

The other party, the appellee, is notified and both parties prepare a brief, or a written statement of the decision. The intention of the brief is to persuade the higher court to make a favoring decision. The appellant seeks to have the case reviewed for legal errors. The appellee wants to see the lower court's decision stand.

Once the judges in higher court make their ruling, the decision is final. Three things can happen. The decision stands, the case is remanded, or moved to a lower court for retrial, or the losing party files a writ of certiorari with the U. S. Supreme for further review. Generally, few writs are granted and only a serious violation of law would warrant a review by this court.

Lesson 8 American Constitution—State and Federal Conflict
Part II
Basic Introduction of American Constitutions
Exercise A

(1) bound

(2) revere

(3) revolutionary

(4) manual

(5) most momentous thing

1. T

2. F

3. F

4. F

5. T

Exercise B

(1) loose treaty, a league, an alliance

(2) frame work

(3) were not really committed

(4) levy taxes

(5) common occurrence

(6) proposes a genuine world government

(7) Martians were coming

How Did American Constitution Come into Being?

Exercise A

1. T

2. F

3. T

4. F

5. F

Exercise B

(1) delegates

(2) notably

(3) fragile union

(4) strengthen this government

(5) strategic ploy

(6) supreme national government

(7) judiciary

Exercise C

1. They came to fix the article of confederation.

2. In the house, there will be representation based on population, giving more power to the larger states. But in the other chamber, each state will have two and only two senators, so in one house, states have proportional power to their size, in the other, they are all made equal.

3. There was no chief of executive, now there will be an elected president. There will be a federal judiciary too, the supreme court.

State and Federal Conflicts

Exercise A

1. F

2. F

Answers

Exercise B

(1) medical marijuana

(2) scrupulous

(3) federal authorities

Marijuana in Harbor Site

Exercise A

1. F

2. T

3. F

Exercise B

1. Harbor site payed over 3 millions dollars taxes last year, we are one of the top 10 tax payers in the city of Oakland and number 2 retail tax payer in the city.

2. Ranges anywhere from cancer, HIV, multiple sclerosis, cerebral palsy, really serious diseases, to more ongoing diseases that may not be so acute, but are chronic.

Part III

1. In the early 1930s, the economy has collapsed, and the country very nearly collapsed along with it.

2. He launched his own revolution, a great experiment he called "the New Deal."

3. stimulate growth and relieve poverty, pension system; controversy and opposition

Part IV

Exercise A

1. F

2. F

3. T

4. T

Exercise B

(1) incentive

(2) justification

(3) economic sense

(4) sulfur dioxide

(5) cross state

(6) 225 years

(7) tug-of-war

Lesson 9 Legal Concepts (1) : Bill of Rights (US)
Part II

1. We can keep our rights and liberties.

2. They were put in there to protect the individual citizen from the government.

The Ten Amendments

The first amendment includes the big three freedoms, freedom of religion, speech and the press.

The second amendment is with its well-regulated militia or the right to keep or bear arms.

The third amendment is entirely devoted to protecting you from having government troops take up residence in your home.

The fourth amendment secures our freedom from unreasonable search and seizure.

The fifth amendment protects you from being tried twice for the same charge or from being forced to testify against yourself.

The six amendment ensures a fair trial of criminal cases.

The seventh amendment guarantees a jury trial in many civil cases.

The eighth amendment protects against cruel and unusual punishment.

The ninth amendment declares that just because certain rights are listed here, it doesn't mean that there are no others.

The tenth amendment says that the power not specifically given to the government in the constitution, are reserved to the states and the people.

Akhil Amar from Yale University

(1) open state conventions

Answers

(2) bottom

(3) epic conversation that electrified the world

(4) Plain

(5) assertions of our rights

Part III

Albert Snider, a Father

1. T

2. T

3. T

4. T

What's Going on with Freedom to Speak

(1) tension

(2) tolerance for unpopular ideas

(3) disloyal language

(4) being arrested or deported

(5) totalitarian enemies

(6) upheld the freedom

(7) controversial

(8) not enforced silence

(9) literally

Human Rights for Prisoner?

Exercise A

1. T

2. F

3. F

4. T

Exercise B

(1) convicted

(2) state penitentiary

(3) 1898

(4) we fight for them

(5) new trial

(6) assured of having a lawyer

Part IV
Exercise A

1. T

2. T

3. F

4. F

Exercise B

(1) aftermath

(2) six amendment protection

(3) legal warrant

(4) self incrimination

(5) remain silent

Lesson 10 Legal Concepts (2): Equal Rights
Part II
Exercise A

1. T

2. F

3. T

4. F

Exercise B

(1) has been left unsettled

(2) contradiction

Answers

(3) ratification

(4) restrict the rights of their former slaves

(5) make certain

Part III

Exercise A

1. F

2. F

3. T

4. F

Exercise B

(1) voting booth

(2) mandated segregation

(3) dared to defy

(4) conscience of the nation

(5) be sacred

Exercise C

2 3 1 5 4

Part IV

Exercise A

1. T

2. T

3. T

4. F

Exercise B

(1) anti-miscegenation law

(2) in their favor

(3) unanimously

(4) infringed

(5) rooted in bigotry

(6) win a majority

(7) prevail

(8) immutable trait

Exercise C

1. A case named "Loving vs. Virginia".

2. The whole purpose of the 14th amendment was to undo that kind of racial discrimination.

3. Women right to vote.

4. Suffrage to anyone over 18.

Part V

Interview with Michelle Alexander

(1) mass incarceration

(2) deemed ineligible

(3) second-class status

(4) are a promise

(5) equal treatment for all

Educational Rights for Illegal Immigrants

Exercise B

1. T

2. F

3. F

4. F

Exercise C

(1) testimony

(2) illegal aliens

(3) dilution of resources

(4) $1,000 per student

(5) privilege

Answers

(6) illegal immigrants

Interview with Professor Armar

1. It lays out the privileges of membership: defining what rights will be protected and who will do the protecting.

2. The original Bill of Rights protects Americans only against Congress; the second Bill of Rights, in effect, against states.

3. Yes, we can say that the 14th Amendment is enforcing a vision of liberty and justice for all.

Lesson 11 Legal Concepts (3) : Constitutional Crisis
Part II
The New Constitutional Construction in Iceland

(1) 300,000

(2) fell apart

(3) The Prime Minister resigned

(4) are engaged in

(5) submit ideas

(6) custom-built

The Development of the Constitution—Historian Rick Beeman

1. T
2. F
3. T

The Development of the Constitution—Professor Akhil Amar
Exercise A

1. T
2. T
3. F
4. F

Exercise B

(1) vast creative white space

(2) democratic idea

(3) Article V

(4) 2/3rds vote

(5) 3/4s of the states

(6) 27 of them

(7) ratified

Part III

Watergate Scandal

Exercise A

1. F

2. F

3. T

4. T

Exercise B

(1) explicitly laid out

(2) Judiciary

(3) break-in

(4) cover-up

(5) special prosecutor

(6) Treason, bribery

(7) entered the fray

(8) impeach

(9) national trauma

Exercise C

(1) defied Congress

(2) intervened

(3) conceived of

Exercise D

1. One reason it worked was that everyone had to obey the rules.

2. The 9 Justices on the Supreme Court are the referees. They make the final calls.

Anti-constitution During Wartime or Crisis

Exercise A

1. T

2. F

3. F

4. T

Exercise B

(1) fragile

(2) precarious balance

(3) led to the internment

(4) desolate camps

(5) posed a threat to

Patriot Act

Exercise A

1. T

2. T

3. F

4. F

Exercise B

(1) fight terrorism

(2) ran afoul of

(3) subjected to

(4) in detention

(5) unsettling

(6) violations

(7) faced controversy

(8) drone attacks

Part IV

1. It is a perennial question. Forever the country has been debating what those clauses mean, and it's still not settled.

2. Yes

Part V

Interview with Rabbi Douglas Sagal

(1) incredibly ancient

(2) 3000

(3) are out there

(4) a living document

Interview with Professor Amar

(1) imperfections

(2) growing and deepening

(3) posterity

(4) what happened in 1787

(5) flawed...spectacular

Lesson 12 Legal Concepts (4): Presumed Innocent

Part II

1. He was charged with housebreaking in 1825, with no one to present him and no witness to call on oath.

2. The trial followed the due process of the day.

3. (1) seismic shifts

   (2) Industrial Revolution

Answers

Development of Lawyer's Role—Garrow's Contribution

Exercise A

1. T
2. T
3. F
4. F

Exercise B

(1) prosecuting criminal cases

(2) facing the death penalty

(3) questioning technique

(4) in felony cases

(5) 1783

(6) prolific defence advocates

Exercise C

(1) in tune with

(2) rigour

(3) take nothing for granted

(4) mere hearsay, was equally admissible

(5) a test of the defendant

(6) proven guilty

Part III

Robert Peel's Contribution to Forgery

Forgery was not the only law needing reform. The whole system, savage and incoherent, required overhauling and only Government could do this. The politician with the courage, the obsessive eye for detail, and the power of personality to take on this project was Robert Peel. When Robert Peel became Home Secretary, there were over 100 statutes dealing with forgery alone. He ruthlessly attacked this legislative mess. 120 statutes were transformed into one, just six pages long. With consummate skill, Robert Peel did more to reform the criminal justice system than almost any other Home Secretary. Over the course of eight years, Peel consolidated three quarters of all offences into a few key Acts. The Waltham Black Act with its dozens of hanging crimes all but disappeared. The death penalty was severely restricted.

Interview with Lord Hurd on Robert Peel's Reform

Exercise A

1. T

2. F

3. F

4. T

Exercise B

1. A riot swept England.

2. Police would not just control people, they would primarily control crime.

3. Because one of the themes which runs through English history in the 18th and 19th century is the fear of a standing army.

Exercise C

(1) deploying police

(2) disperse within an hour

(3) death

(4) 1829

(5) control crime

(6) deterrent against crime

(7) draconian penalties

Part IV

Exercise A

1. The only means of deterring crime was through exemplary punishment-whipping, transportation and hanging.

2. Yes.

Answers

3. An outbreak of jail fever promiscuously killed 60 people, including two judges and the Lord Mayor.

4. Yes.

5. Over 200 crimes.

Exercise B

(1) from start to verdict

(2) was entitled to

(3) unfamiliar procedures and terminology

(4) lengthy day

(5) judicial lassitude

Lesson 13 Laying Down the Law—English Common Law
Part II
Exercise A

1. The danger is that it can make the law seem far removed from most people's lives.

2. The public.

3. Pioneering and courageous individuals.

Exercise B

(1) precedent

(2) fairness and equality

(3) England's people

(4) being forged

(5) guilty of brutality and excess

(6) exceeds

The Origin of the English Common Law
Exercise A

(1) track down

(2) 5th

(3) Anglo-Saxon kingdom

(4) testify

(5) enormous importance

(6) dating back to 600

(7) beginning of English literature

(8) injuries, wrongs

Exercise B

1. There are four ranks, which are the King, the aristocracy, the ordinary free man, and the slave.

2. The rank of the victim.

3. On the families, the relatives, the victims.

Exercise C

(1) are bound to have suited

(2) solely based on

(3) settle a dispute

(4) draw a line under a grievance

(5) internal feuds

(6) escalating conflicts

Part III

The Vicissitude of Law

1. The next step is having institutions to administer and implement them.

2. The shire courts, forerunners of our county courts.

3. On oaths.

4. Your social status and the nature of the alleged offence.

5. 36.

The Later Anglo-Saxons Age

1. The threat of death or mutilation.

2. Determining proof.

Answers

3. The first involved carrying a piece of red-hot iron in your bare hand; the second is that you were bound and lowered into a body of sanctified water.

4. Sinking indicated innocence. Floating was proof of guilt.

Interview with Professor John Hudson

1. A way of settling cases that you couldn't settle in other ways.

2. A way of trying to scare people either into confessing or very often into settling.

3. 50%.

4. What convicts you, it seems, in England, is not whether you're burnt or not—everyone would be burnt—it's whether your hand is clean or foul.

5. The clergy.

The End of Anglo-Saxons Age; Norman Empire

Exercise A

1. T

2. F

3. T

4. F

Exercise B

1. From 1135 to 1154.

2. Nothing less than the father of the English common law.

3. Making sure that the law was being enforced by the shire courts and claiming all the fines that were due to the King.

Exercise C

(1) ensure their common, consistent and effective implementation

(2) roving Royal Justices

(3) hand-picked officials

(4) Earl

(5) demise

(6) shake down

213

Part IV

1. The king was about to put his seal on a document—the Great Charter, Magna Carta.

2. John's disastrous French wars, his repeated demands for money, and his abuse of royal courts to levy fines.

3. It was a groundbreaking recognition that the English people had rights. No free man shall be seized or imprisoned. Etc.

4. The origin of fundamental civil liberties.

Lesson 14 The Pursuit of Liberty—English Common Law
Part II

1. At midnight on May 11th, 1640.

2. Treason.

3. Yes.

4. One of England's greatest civil libertarians was banished there.

Star Chamber

(1) its variety

(2) do justice

(3) The common law

(4) royal prerogative

(5) beyond justice

(6) bribed or intimidated

(7) interrogated, and judged

Corrupted Star Chamber

1. T

2. T

3. F

4. T

Part III

Petition of Rights

1. T

2. F

3. F

4. T

5. F

Petition's Crisis

(1) lighting of bonfires

(2) plotting his next move

(3) dissolved

(4) resorted to

(5) clamp down

(6) dissent

Part IV

1. Charles' refusal to accept that he did not have a divine right to dictate the law of the land.

2. Parliament, over 80000.

3. By being instructed by solicitors.

4. Cab rank rule.

Lesson 15 International Business Law

Part II

Exercise A

1. 法官

2. 当事人

3. 判决

4. 法庭

5. 法庭

6. 审议

7. 文件，文书

8. 除……之外

9. 审讯，听审

Exercise B

1. a—c

2. a—g

3. a—h

Part III

International Law

Exercise A

(1) legal rules and norms

(2) beyond

(3) public

(4) private

(5) individuals

(6) nongovernmental

(7) confused with

(8) conflicts of laws

(9) goodwill

(10) civility

Exercise B

1. Because nations and individuals regard international law as law, it is law.

2. The subject matter of international law has changed dramatically in recent years. Traditionally, international law governed state-state relationships.

3. Comity is not law because countries do not regard it as something they are required to respect.

Answers

What Is International Business Law?

International business law refers to the body of rules and norms regulating international business transactions and the relationships between business organizations across national boundaries. It focuses on the business activities conducted between individuals and enterprises from different countries. By contrast, international economic law is thought to be in the scope of public international law, it deals primarily with the rights and duties of states and intergovernmental organizations in their international business, economic, affairs, and business entities. Nevertheless, in a broad sense, international economic law encompasses both the conduct of sovereign states in international economic relations, and the conduct of private parties involved in cross-border economic and business transactions as well.

Part IV

What Are the Sources of International Law?

1. International treaties or conventions, whether general or particular, establishing rules expressly recognized by the contesting states;
2. International custom, as an evidence of a general practice accepted as law, it consists of two parts: States practice and opinion of juries;
3. Judicial decisions and the teaching of the most highly qualified publicists of the various nations, as subsidiary means of the determination of rules of law;
4. The general principles of law recognized by civilized nations.

What Is Common Law? What Are the Differences Between Civil Law and Common Law?

The law of the land which comes from neither the statute books nor the constitution, but from court law reports.

Originally that body of law which was common to all parts of England was not customary or local law and developed over centuries from the English courts to be adopted and further developed in countries using that system. As compared to democratically maintained law, common law is judge maintained and modified law and is valid unless it conflicts with statute law.

Common law also known as case law or precedent is law developed by judges, courts, and similar tribunals, stated in decisions that nominally decide individual cases but that in addition have precedential effect on future cases.

The common-law system prevails in England, the United States, and other countries colonized by England. It is distinct from the civil-law system, which predominates in Europe and in areas colonized by France and Spain. The common-law system is used in all the states of the United States except Louisiana, where French Civil Law combined with English Criminal Law to form a hybrid system. The common-law system is also used in Canada, except in the Province of Quebec, where the French civil-law system prevails.

Part V

1. Firstly, their parties are different. International law deals with three kinds of international relationships:

    (1) Those between states and states;

    (2) Those between states and persons;

    (3) Those between persons and persons. However, domestic law deals with relationships among natural persons, companies and enterprises.

    Besides, their forms are also different to each other. Domestic law usually appears as enacted law and case law. But international law usually appears as customs, treaties and legislation.

2. We can still distinguish them by their definition. Treaties are legally binding agreements between two or more states. Conventions are legally binding agreements between states sponsored by international organizations, such as the United Nations.

3. Some rules have been around for such a long time or are so generally accepted that they are described as customary law. To show that a customary practice has become customary law, two elements must be established—one behavioral and one psychological. The first—called uses in Latin—requires consistent and recurring action (or lack of action if the custom is one of noninvolvement) by states. The psychological element in showing

that a customary practice has become law is the requirement that states observing the custom must it as binding.

4. General Assembly; the Security Council; the Secretariat; the International Court of Justice; the Trusteeship Council; the Economic; Social Council.

5. There are some famous organs of the United Nations. One of the most famous important intergovernmental organization is European Union (EU) . Founded in 1951 by 6 states (Belgium, France, Germany, Italy, Luxembourg, and the Netherlands), its member states increased to 9 in 1973 (with the addition of Denmark, Ireland, and the United Kingdom). The EU already has a population of nearly half a billion, the largest population in the world after China and India. The main institutions of the EU are the European Commission, the Council of the European Union, the European Parliament, and the European Court of Justice.

6. International law looks upon individuals in two different ways: (1) it ignores them or (2) it treats them as its subjects. The traditional view is to ignore them. This is based on the idea that international law (or, more particularly, the law of nations) applies only to states. Some writers still believe that this is the only proper way for international law to treat individuals.

Part VI

Reference:

HOLDING: No.

LAW: Import restrictions to protect human life and health are allowed "if that objective cannot be achieved by measures less restrictive of intra-Community trade." Council Directive 79/112 allows Member States to have "detailed rules for the labelling of foodstuffs offered for sale to the ultimate consumer without pre-packaging" for purposes of consumer protection and avoiding confusion. "National measures may not conflict with... the fundamental principles of the Community—in this case of the free movement of goods—unless they are justified by reasons recognized by Community law."

EXPLANATION: Germany's explanations for the Meat Regulation are rejected as not complying with its treaty obligations under Article 30 of the EEC Treaty, which provides, "Quantitative restrictions on imports and all measures having equivalent effect shall, without prejudice to the following provisions, be prohibited between member States."

ORDER: The declaration is made that Germany failed to fulfil its EEC Treaty obligations under Article 30.

Lesson 16 Business Organization Law
Part II
Exercise A

business structure, business name, capital, business scope, principal place of business, partner(s), market research, consulting a industry veteran/lawyer/accountant, feasibility study, learn relevant regulations and policies, business plan, partnership agreement, etc.

Exercise B

1. sole proprietorship

2. general partnership

3. limited partnership

4. limited liability company

5. nonprofit corporation

6. corporation

7. franchise

8. joint venture

Part III
Exercise A

1. legal entities, litigation

2. over 75%, less paperwork

3. sell shares, stockholders

Answers

4. C corporation, S corporation

5. pass through taxation, personal tax return

Exercise B

1. Because there is a lot less paperwork on a yearly basis to deal with in the simple fact you can always convert a limited liability company to a corporation.

2. Corporations are more complicated because they have different requirements and filings with the Secretary of State's office every year. Another important thing to consider is you can never go from a corporation and convert it back to a limited liability company, you can only go from a limited liability company to a corporation.

3. Corporations are invaluable if you plan in the future on trading your company on the stock exchange or what is known is going public.

How Is a Corporation Like a Person?

If a corporation is legally a person, then states cannot limit corporate rights without due process of law either. At first, corporations were not fully recognized as persons. But Jeff Sklansky at Oregon State University said that changed. He said the general direction of the Supreme Court and the federal courts was to recognize corporations as persons with the same Fourteenth Amendment rights as individuals. Yet corporations have a right that real people do not: limited liability. For example, a corporation can face civil or criminal fines and individual lawbreakers can go to jail. But limited liability means the actions of a corporation are not the responsibility of its shareholders. Jeff Sklansky says the nineteenth century development of limited liability helped shape the modern corporation.

Part IV

Piercing the Corporate Veil

If you're an owner of a corporation, then you know that one of the greatest advantages to this business model is the personal liability protection. Corporations are independent entities in the eyes of the law, meaning that any losses, liabilities or debts belong only to the corporation, and not to the individual owners. If the corporation is subjected to a multi-million dollar lawsuit verdict, for example, then only the corporate assets may be used to satisfy the judgment, not the personal assets of the individual owners. Yet in limited circumstances, the court will find that this liability protection should not apply and will pierce the corporate veil, this allowing plaintiffs or debtors to recover damages from the personal assets of the corporation owners as well as corporation itself. Generally, the corporate veil may be pierced if the corporation was just a show for the owners' individual acts. "For the owners' individual acts, with the owners intentionally use their business to commit a wrong for act." Piercing the corporate veil is a matter of state law, and each state has its own precise rules for applying these doctrines.

What Is a Multinational Corporation?

A multinational corporation is a business that has its facilities and other assets in at least one country other than its home country. Such companies have offices and/or factories in different countries and usually have a centralized head office where they co-ordinate global management.

Generally, any company or group that derives a quarter of its revenue from operations outside of its home country is considered a multinational corporation.

There are four categories of multinational corporations: (1) a multinational, decentralized corporation with strong home country presence; (2) a global, centralized corporation that acquires cost advantage through centralized production wherever cheaper resources are available; (3) an international company that builds on the parent corporation's technology or R&D; or (4) a transnational enterprise that combines the previous three approaches. According to UN data, some 35,000 companies have direct investment in foreign countries, and the largest 100 of them control about 40 percent of world trade.

In economic terms, a firm's advantages in establishing a multinational corporation include both vertical and horizontal economies of scale and an increased market share. Although cultural barriers can create unpredictable obstacles as companies establish offices and production plants around the world, a firm's technical expertise, experienced personnel, and proven strategies usually can be transferred from country to country. Critics of the multinational corporation usually view it as an economic and, often, political means

Answers

of foreign domination.

Part V

1. (1) The Capital of a Sole Proprietorship is contributed by one person.

    (2) The Business of a Sole Proprietorship is controlled by its sole owner.

    (3) The Profits and Losses of a Sole Proprietorship are assumed by its sole owner.

    Advantage: Convenient formation and flexible management.

    Disadvantages: Higher business risks and restricted business scales.

2. A designation for the partnership and the names of the partners;

    The nature and scope of the partnership business;

    The method for and amount of making capital contribution by each partner;

    The methods for profit distribution and loss allocation;

    The operation and management of the partnership business;

    The duration of the partnership;

    Other provisions, if necessary.

3. Internal Relation of a Partnership:

    Rights of partners: (1) Right of Sharing Profits; (2) Right of Management; (3) Right of Compensation; (4) Right of Supervising and Managing Partnership Account.

    Duties of partners: (1) Duty to Make Capital Contributions; (2) Duty to Loyalty; (3) Duty to Care; (4) Duty of Not Transferring His Capital Contributions Discretionarily.

    External Relation of a Partnership: (1) Carry on the partnership business, bind the partnership and the other partners; (2) Any restriction may not be asserted as a defense against a third person without knowledge of such restriction; (3) The partnership shall be liable for the wrongful acts and has rights to claim compensation for losses; (4) New partners shall not be liable for the debts incurred before he joins the partnership.

4. Branch is a unit or part of a company. It's not separately incorporated. While subsidiary is a company owned by parent or a parent's holding company. Unlike a branch, it's separately incorporated.

5. Agent is an independent person or company with authority to act on behalf of the

enterprise. While representative office is a contact point where interested parties can obtain information about the company, it does not conduct business for the company.

6. By purchasing a franchise, you often can sell goods and services that have instant name recognition and can obtain training and ongoing support to help you succeed. But be cautious. Like any investment, purchasing a franchise is not a guarantee of success. There are strong contracts in place that should be considered fully before investing in a franchise.

Part VI
Reference:

HOLDING: Yes.

LAW: Defamation does not occur at the time of publication or where a web server resides, but when a third party reads the publication and thinks less of the plaintiff.

EXPLANATION: United States law is friendly to commercial media, and defendant's position would give it a financial advantage, to "the serious disadvantage of those unfortunate enough to be reputationally damaged outside the United States." A multinational business cannot expect to ignore the laws of other nations. "The fact that publication might occur everywhere does not mean that it occurs nowhere."

ORDER: Dow Jones' appeal is dismissed with costs.

Lesson 17 International Commercial Arbitration
Part II
Exercise A

1.–10.: (√)

Exercise B

(1) There shall be an arbitration agreement;

(2) There shall be a specific appeal request, facts and reasons for the appeal;

(3) The case shall be within the jurisdictional power of the arbitration commission.

Answers

Part III

Exercise A

(1) hearing

(2) arbitrator

(3) decision

(4) precedent

(5) conciliation

(6) enforceable

(7) compel

(8) impose his award

(9) globalization

(10) arbitration clauses

Exercise B

1. The arbitrator's decision is binding only on the parties to the dispute, and is not a legal precedent, as is a judicial ruling.

2. All the three involve a third party who transmits and interprets the proposals of the parties and sometimes advances independent proposals. Mediation does not always result in a settlement agreement. It lacks the procedural and constitutional protections guaranteed by the federal and state courts. Legal precedent cannot be set in mediation and it has no formal discovery process. Conciliation is based on formal discovery process, while a conciliator is not so powerful as the arbitrator, whose arbitration results in a binding and enforceable award, he cannot compel the parties to reach a settlement and still he has no power to impose his award on the parties.

3. In order to avoid the potential costs, delays, and uncertainties of litigation in foreign courts.

Advantages of Arbitration

Parties often seek to resolve their disputes through arbitration because of a number of perceived potential advantages over judicial proceeding. First, when the subject matter of the dispute is highly technical, arbitrators with an appropriate degree of expertise can be appointed. Second, arbitration is often more efficient than litigation in court; arbitration can be cheaper and more flexible for businesses. Third, arbitral proceeding and an arbitral award are general non-pubic, and can be made confidential. In addition, arbitration offers the parties the opportunity to choose their own arbitrator, and in arbitral proceedings the language of arbitration may be chosen. Because of the provisions of the New York Convention 1958, arbitration award are generally easier to enforce in other nations than court judgments. And in most legal systems there are very limited avenues for appeal of an arbitral award, which is sometimes an advantage because it limits the duration of the dispute and any associated liability.

Part IV

International Arbitration

International arbitration has been one of the preferred means of dispute resolution for the past 10th of centuries. It goes as far back as uniform tablets in what's modern-day era extending through the trade fairs in the Middle Ages up until the present day. International arbitration today is essentially global. The New York Convention adopted in 1958 was a hundred and fifty-six contracting states around the world. The insert role model law on international commercial arbitration is its counterpart together they provide a global constitution for international arbitration. International arbitration is used to resolve a host of disputes today.

It's used for international business disputes. It's used for investment disputes between host states and foreign investors. It's employed for sports for tax for maritime disputes. Parties from every geographic region of the globe use international arbitration to resolve their most complex and most important disputes. Parties use international arbitration because it's expert, efficient and enforceable. Arbitration is expert because the parties choose arbitrators who are precisely suited to the circumstances of their dispute. Arbitration is efficient because the tribunal runs the proceedings expeditiously and cheaply. And arbitration is enforceable because of the New York Convention and UNCITRAL Model

Law.

International arbitration is the subject of intense contemporary debate. The proper role of investment arbitration and bilateral on investment treaties is the subject we read about in the front pages of the business section most days of the week. The allocation of authority between arbitral tribunals and national courts is debated among national parliaments and arbitral institutions around the world. The past four decades have witnessed an explosive growth in international arbitration as well as in the issues that it raises. One never knows what the future will bring but we would expect that it will bring even greater growth in international arbitration and even more interest in the issues that it raises.

International Commercial Arbitration Explained

Commercial international arbitration is an alternative dispute resolution where the disputing parties agreed to appoint an impartial arbitrator based on his expertise and reputation to decide a commercial dispute by means of a final and binding in award. Arbitration is considered to be international when the party's facts or the legal matter extend beyond the single jurisdiction. The distinction between domestic and international arbitration is important as it will affect the enforcement of the award. On the other hand, arbitration differs from other types of dispute resolutions as the arbitrator is selected by the parties and unlike mediation and conciliation, the arbitrator not only resolves the dispute but he also makes a binding decision.

Arbitration disputes usually arise from a variety of business deals such as merger and acquisition, financial services, construction and infrastructure, intellectual property and purchase and sale agreements. Arbitration is chosen by the parties because it offers the following benefits over local state courts. First, the parties are free to select the place of the arbitration. Second, the arbitrator is neutral, independent and impartial party, which means an unbiased dispute resolution. Third, the proceedings are conducted in private and confidential manner. Furthermore, the arbitration award is final with no right of appeal, which saves the party's time and money when compared to court's lengthy appellate proceedings. Finally, the cross-border acceptance of an arbitration award is supported by international treaties . As a result, the arbitration award can be easily enforced abroad unlike a foreign court judgment.

However, despite being fast and effective, arbitration can have the following disadvantages. First, the arbitration technical nature can lead to delays and uncertain results. Second, the arbitrator power is limited as he cannot order preemptive injunctions, which can be only granted by the state courts. The arbitration confidentiality causes a lack of transparency, which makes the process subject to buyers. In addition, when the losing party does not comply with the award, the enforcement relys on the state court held where confidentiality is lost. The finality of the arbitration award means that a wrong decision cannot be corrected nor appealed. In addition, arbitration is expensive, especially the arbitrator fees and expert technical reports. And lastly, arbitration may not be suitable where there are several parties to a dispute like in projects and construction claims where a single dispute may involve different companies working on the same deal.

Part V

1. Domestic arbitration institutions: China International Economic & Trade Arbitration Commission (CIETAC), China Maritime Arbitration Commission (CMAC), Hong Kong International Arbitration Center (HKIAC), Singapore International Arbitration Center (SIAC);

   International arbitration institutions: American Arbitration Association (AAA), London Court of International Arbitration (LCIA), Arbitration Institute of the Stockholm Chamber of Commerce (SCC), International Chamber of Commerce (ICC), International Centre for Settlement of Investment Disputes (ICSID) .

2. There are two basic types of arbitration agreement: an agreement to submit future disputes to arbitration; an agreement to submit existing disputes to arbitration.

3. Functions of arbitration agreement: Preclude the Jurisdiction of court; Impose on the parties the duty of arbitration.

4. The compulsory contents include: The parties' intention to settle a particular dispute

through arbitration, the scope of the arbitration, the arbitral institution. There are some optional contents which may include: arbitral procedure rules, selection of arbitrators, payment of arbitrator fees, Situs.

5. (1) File a Claim: A claimant initiates an arbitration by filing a statement of claim that specifies the relevant facts and remedies requested. (2) Answer a Claim: A respondent responds to an arbitration claim by filing an answer that specifies the relevant facts and available defenses to the statement of claim. (3) Arbitrator Selection: Arbitrator selection is the process in which the parties receive lists of potential arbitrators and select the panel to hear their case. (4) Prehearing Conferences: Prior to the hearing, the arbitrators and parties meet telephonically to schedule hearing dates and resolve preliminary issues. (5) Discovery: Discovery is the exchange of documents and information in preparation for the hearing. (6) Hearings: The parties and arbitrators meet in person to conduct the hearing in which the parties present arguments and evidence in support of their respective cases. (7) Decision & Awards: After the conclusion of the hearing, the arbitrators deliberate the facts of the case and render a written decision called an award.

6. (1) Time limits (often short); (2) Lack precedent and uniformity, quality varies; (3) Lack of proper notice of the appointment of arbitrator or arbitral proceedings or otherwise unable to present case; (4) Award deals with matters not contemplated by or falling within the terms of the submission to arbitration; (5) Composition of the arbitral authority or the arbitral procedure was not in accordance with the agreement of the parties; (6) Subject matter of dispute is not capable of being settled by arbitration; (7) The recognition or enforcement of the award would be contrary to the public policy of that country.

Part VI

Reference:

HOLDING: No.

LAW: NAFTA Article 1105(1) provides: "Each party shall accord to investments of investors of another party treatment in accordance with international law, including fair and equitable treatment and full protection and security."

EXPLANATION: The three-member tribunal stated that "the whole trial and... verdict were clearly improper and cannot be squared with minimum standards of international law and fair and equitable treatment." However, Loewen failed to exhaust its remedies in the US judicial system. Loewen did not state why they chose to settle instead of pursuing an appeal to the US Supreme Court.

ORDER: Loewen's claim is denied.

Lesson 18 The Dispute Settlement System of WTO
Part II
Exercise A

> T: (1) (2) (3) (4) (6) (7) (8) (9)
> F: (5) (10)

Exercise B

International Court of Justice

International Criminal Court

World Trade Organization Dispute Settlement of Investment Disputes

Other Arbitration Tribunals

Part III
Exercise A

(1) implementing

(2) enforcing

(3) panelists

(4) involved

(5) decision

(6) Appellate Body

(7) resolve

(8) consultation

Answers

(9) assistance

(10) negotiations

Exercise B

1. Its main function is to ensure that trade flows as smoothly, predictably and freely as possible.

2. The organs charged with carrying out the DSU are the Dispute Settlement Body, the Dispute Settlement Panels, and the Appellate Body.

3. Its function is to assist the DSB by making an objective assessment of the facts and determining the applicability and conformity with WTO agreements, then making findings to help the DSB make recommendations and rulings.

The Dispute Settlement Understanding

The current dispute settlement system was created as part of the WTO Agreement during the Uruguay Round. It is embodied in the Understanding on Rules and Procedures Governing the Settlement of Disputes, commonly referred to as the Dispute Settlement Understanding and abbreviated "DSU" (referred to as such in this guide). The DSU, which constitutes Annex 2 of the WTO Agreement, sets out the procedures and rules that define today's dispute settlement system. It should however be noted that, to a large degree, the current dispute settlement system is the result of the evolution of rules, procedures and practices developed over almost half a century under the GATT 1947.

Part IV

GATT and WTO — Social Studies

Open. Understand the vital role of the dispute settlement system in WTO.

WTO Accused of Failing to Assist Developing Nations

The World Trade Organization must deliver on its promise to knock down trade barriers. It has failed to assist developing nations who stand to gain most from access to markets in more industrialized nations, which impacts current trade policies on farmers.

Part V

1. A unified process that applies to all disputes arising under WTO agreements.

2. The DSB is made up of three panelists unless the parties agree within ten days of its establishment that it should consist of five panelists.

3. It is responsible for establishing panels, adopting their reports and those of the Appellate Body, monitoring the implementation of rulings and recommendations, and authorizing the suspension of concessions and other member state privileges.

4. The Appellate Body is an appeals board made up of seven persons, three of whom will serve on any one case.

5. Famous WTO agreements include the General Agreement on Tariffs and Trade (GATT), the General Agreement on Trade in Services (GATS), and the Agreement on Trade Related Aspects of Intellectual Property (TRIPS). GATT is now the WTO's principal rule-book for trade in goods.

6. The rulings of Panel and Appellate Body have no formal precedential effect. That is, both the Panels and the Appellate Body may rely on their own earlier legal rulings, but they are also free to deviate from those rulings as they think necessary.

Part VI

Reference:

HOLDING: No.

LAW/EXPLANATION: The Vienna Convention on the Law of Treaties, Art. 31(3)(b) states that "any subsequent practice in the application of the treaty which establishes the agreement of the parties regarding its interpretation" is to be "taken into account together with the context" in interpreting the terms of the treaty. Under GATT 1947, a panel report was binding on the parties to the dispute, but subsequent panels were not legally bound by the details and reasoning of a previous panel report. Additionally, the GATT 1947 Contracting Parties did not adopt the legal reasoning of a panel report when they adopted its conclusions and recommendations. The provisions of the WTO Agreement and its Annex 1A "bring the legal history and experience under the GATT 1947 into the new realm of the WTO in a way that ensures continuity." Adopted panel reports, therefore, are an important part of the acquired interpretation of the GATT. "They create legitimate expectations among WTO members, and... should be taken into account where they are relevant to any dispute. However, they are not binding, except with respect to resolving the particular dispute between the parties to that dispute."

ORDER: The Panel erred in its conclusion.

Lesson 19 International Center for Settlement of Investment Disputes
Part II

Exercise A

The World Bank's goal is to reduce poverty and to improve the living standards of the people in low and middle-income countries. The World Bank is one of the world's largest sources of funding and knowledge to support governments of member countries in their efforts to invest in schools and health centers provide water and electricity, fight disease and protect the environment.

Exercise B

Its five agencies are: (1) International Bank for Reconstruction and Development (IBRD) (国际复兴开发银行); (2) International Development Association (IDA) (国际开发协会) (3) International Finance Corporation (IFC) (国际金融公司); (4) Multilateral Investment Guarantee Agency (MIGA) (多边投资担保机构); (5) International Centre for Settlement of Investment Disputes (ICSID) (国际投资争端解决中心).

Part III
Exercise A

1. international arbitration, conciliation

2. 159, governing

3. Panel of Arbitrators, Panel of Conciliators

4. secretary-general, registrar

5. diverse, decision-makers

Exercise B

1. The purpose of establishment shall be to provide facilities for conciliation and arbitration of investment disputes, to encourage international flow of investment and mitigate non-commercial risks.
2. The ICSID, has an Administrative Council, a Secretariat, and two panels of experts.
3. The most important basic rule established by the Washington Convention is that third-party stated, including the state of the investor involved in the dispute, are not allowed to intervene.

Constituting an ICSID Arbitration Tribunal

Jurisdiction of the Centre shall extend to any legal dispute arising directly out of an investment. Before ICSID can set up a tribunal to resolve a particular dispute, there are some prerequisites: First, the state where the investment is being made (the host state) and the state of which the investor is a national (the home state) must both be parties to the Washington Convention. Second, the host state must have notified ICSID of the class or classes of disputes that it considers arbitrable. Third, the investor and the host state must both consent to ICSID jurisdiction. These prerequisites may not be waived. Also, once consent has been given to set up the tribunal, unilateral withdrawal is ineffective.

Part IV

Investment Arbitration

Open. This video is about Investment Arbitration in Asia. The pros and cons of transparency, confidentiality. The future of Investment Arbitration in Asia.

The Importance of Diversity in Investment Arbitration

Open. Justin D'Agostino, Global Head of Dispute Resolution, Herbert Smith Freehills talks to Conventus Law about the importance of diversity when it comes to solving international disputes.

Part V

1. First, the state wherein the investment is being made(the host state) and the state of which the investor is a national(the home state) must both be parties to the Washington

Answers

Convention. Second, the investor and the host state must both consent to ICSID jurisdiction.

2. By giving consent to ICSID arbitration, the litigants are deemed to have excluded all other remedies. The case cannot be tried in a municipal or another international tribunal, nor can the investor ask its home state for diplomatic protection. Note: The host state can require that all local remedies be exhausted before the dispute can be taken to ICSID.

3. General Requirements: The ICSID Convention provides guidance as to who may be designated to the Panel of Arbitrators and of Conciliators and serve in arbitration and conciliation proceedings. The Additional Facility Rules contain corresponding provisions concerning the required qualifications. These stipulate that all ICSID arbitrators, conciliators and ad hoc Committee members be persons: (1) of high moral character; (2) with recognized competence in the fields of law, commerce, industry or finance; and (3) who may be relied upon to exercise independent judgment. In addition, the ICSID Convention and Additional Facility Rules contain certain nationality requirements applicable to each arbitration case. A majority of arbitrators on a Tribunal must be nationals of States other than the State party to the dispute and the State whose national is a party to the dispute.

4. The litigants may agree to any number, but if they want more than one, the number must be odd.

5. The IBRD aims to reduce poverty in middle-income and creditworthy poorer countries. The IFC offers investment, advisory, and asset management services to encourage private sector development in developing countries. The IDA focuses on supporting the world's poorest countries. The MIGA offers political risk insurance and credit enhancement guarantees. The ICSID is an international arbitration institution which facilitates legal dispute resolution and conciliation between international investors.

6. (1) The parties may agree on the use of one or two languages to be used in the proceeding, provided that, if they agree on any language that is not an official language

of the Centre, the Commission, after consultation with the Secretary-General, gives its approval. If the parties do not agree on any such procedural language, each of them may select one of the official languages (i. e., English, French and Spanish) for this purpose. (2) If two procedural languages are selected by the parties, any instrument may be filed in either language. Either language may be used at the hearings, subject, if the Commission so requires, to translation and interpretation. The recommendations and the report of the Commission shall be rendered and the record kept in both procedural languages, both versions being equally authentic.

Part VI
Reference:

HOLDING: Yes!

LAW: ICSID Convention Art. 72, a state party cannot withdraw by filling a later reservation to the convention or even by denouncing the convention.

EXPLANATION: Plaintiff and defendant both are the parties to the Washington Convention and both consent to ICSID jurisdiction constituting an ICSID Arbitration Tribunal. An arbitration agreement has been made before the defendant's new government cancelled all tax holidays. According to Article 72, the defendant cannot deliberately avoid the obligation under the agreement.

ORDER: The tribunal have jurisdiction to proceed.

Lesson 20 Protection of Intellectual Property
Part II
Exercise A

1. d   2. b   3. a   4. f   5. j   6. h   7. c   8. e   9. i   10. g

Answers

Exercise B

> Intellectual property, industrial property, inventions (patents), trademarks, industrial designs, geographic indicators of source, copyright, literary works, artistic works, novels, poems, plays and films, musical works, drawings, paintings , photographs and sculptures, architectural designs

Part III

What Is Intellectual Property?

Exercise A

1. intangible personal property, providing protection

2. crucial, rules

3. monopoly, a product or process

4. exclusive, original

5. restrain, trade secrets

Exercise B

1. It could be said that all IP rights have two common characteristics: first, all are related to a form of intellectual achievement or activity; and second, all are rights as recognized and protected by a particular law.

2. The basic objectives for granting this right are: to inform the public through publication of details from the application of the latest technological advances; to provide an incentive for innovation and thereby stimulate economic activity; and to provide a reward for creative and innovative effort.

3. The rights in the trademark are based on use and goodwill in common law.

What Are the Types of Infringement of Intellectual Property?

Maybe the most striking infringement of intellectual property in our everyday life is the piracy. We are exposed to an age never knowing a world without Software Piracy, CD Piracy, Book Piracy, etc. But that is not what the infringement of intellectual property is all about. It actually includes patent infringement, copyright infringement, trademark infringement. Infringement of a patent consists of the unauthorized making, using, offering for sale or selling any patented invention during the term of the patent. Copyright infringement occurs when a person copies someone else's copyright items without permission. This would also include public display of a copy of copyrighted work. As for trademark infringement, the use of a trademark in connection with the sale of a good constitutes infringement. For example, the use of an identical mark on the same product would clearly constitute infringement.

Part IV

Basic Facts— Trademarks, Patents, and Copyrights

This video provides a quick and easy breakdown of the three main types of intellectual property: trademarks, patents, and copyrights. You'll learn how trademarks differ from domain names and business names. By the end of the video, you'll understand how to use each type of intellectual property to protect a different aspect of your business.

New IP Threat to Foreign Companies in China

International businesses operating in China may now be subject to the same Internet security as other Chinese, putting their intellectual property at high risk.

The Quality Brands Protection Committee oversees intellectual property rights of companies operating in China. CNN reports the Committee has sent an email to over 200 members, warning them they may be approached by Chinese authorities. They reported some of their clients were forced to buy and install Internet monitoring software. Up until now, many international companies sidestep the great firewall by having their own networks.

CNN interviewed Thomas Parenty, an information security specialist. He says that the software is essentially a Trojan horse that would allow the Chinese authorities to spy on international company's networks. He told CNN, quote "If you're concerned about IP (intellectual property), you might as well roll up your tents because it's essentially game over." So far only a handful of companies reported being approached by Chinese police. Those who were confronted were either forced to install the Internet logging software or were asked to be inspected. CNN reports that local officials threatened to cut off their service and fine them if they did not comply.

Part V

1. Intellectual property is, in essence, useful information or knowledge. For the purposes of study, it can be divided into two principal branches: artistic property and industrial property.

    Artistic property encompasses artistic, literary, and musical works. These are protected, in most countries, by copyrights and neighboring rights.

    Industrial property is itself divided into two categories: inventions and trademarks. Inventions include both useful products and useful manufacturing processes. They are protected in a variety of ways, the most common protection being in the form of patents, petty patents, and inventors' certificates.

2. A copyright holder typically has exclusive rights: (1) to make and sell copies of the work (including typically, electronic copies), (2) to import or export the work, (3) to make derivative works, (4) to publicly perform the work, (5) to sell or assign these rights to others.

3. Yes, the protection is usually given for a finite term (typically 20 years in the case of patents) .

4. From the perspective of an owner, a trademark is the right to put a product protected by the mark into circulation for the first time.

    From the perspective of a consumer, a trademark serves to (1) designate the origin or source of a product or service, (2) indicate a particular standard of quality, (3) represent the goodwill of the manufacturer, (4) protect the consumers from confusion.

5. Trademarks are acquired in two ways: by use and by registration. Except for Canada and the Philippines, in the rest of the world, a mark can be registered even if it has never been used in commerce.

6. The Berne Convention; The Agreement on Trade-Related Aspects of Intellectual Property Rights (TRIPs Agreement) ; The Paris Convention for the Protection of Industrial Property in 1878.

Part VI
Reference:

Google's way raises questions of copyright infringement. *New York Times Magazine* can file a lawsuit against Google for its infringement. *New York Times Magazine* is an university press, it is a not-for-profit. But the way Google's going about it, the scanning of the books at the libraries—that doesn't seem to be fair. They're not asking the press's permission to scan those books. They're giving a copy of everything that they scan to the libraries that are participating, and that, of course, means less revenue for the press, which hurts their bottom line and makes it less likely they'll be able to publish scholarship in the future.

Normal copyright has always required that permission is requested by the person who wants to make the copy. Google hasn't asked for permission here.

Lesson 21 United Nations Convention on Contracts for the International Sale of Goods
Part II
Exercise A

Case 1: Going shopping: the goods are placed on the shelves (invitation for offer) ; the customer picks up the desired goods (offer) ; the customer makes payment (acceptance).

Case 2: Taking taxi: Opinion 1: the taxi is vacant or available(offer); the passenger waves his hand to the taxi (acceptance). Opinion 2: the taxi is vacant (invitation for offer); waving to the taxi (offer); boarding the taxi (acceptance).

Case 3: Auction: public announcement (invitation for offer) ; making bid (bidding) by potential buyers (offer) ; fall of hammer (acceptance).

Exercise B

The seller's basic obligation is to deliver the goods, hand over any documents and ensure the ownership of the goods and the conformity of the goods with the contract.

The main obligation of the buyer is to pay for the price and to take delivery of the goods.

Part III

Exercise A

1. addressed, to be bound

2. invitations, contrary

3. irrevocable, dispatches

4. promise, enforceable

5. statement, assent

Exercise B

1. The proposal must be sufficiently definite to describe the goods and state or provides a means for determining the quantity and the price.

2. An offer becomes effective only after it reaches the offeree.

3. A contract comes into existence at the point in time when an offer is accepted.

Transactions Covered in CISG

CISG applies if the following conditions are met: first, the contract is for the commercial sale of goods; second, it is between parties whose places of business are in different states, that is, nationality or citizenship of individuals is not a determining factor; the parties to a contract may exclude or modify the CISG's application by a "choice of law" clause. Whether parties can exclude a domestic law and adopt the CISG in its place depends on the rules of the state where the case is heard. CISG does not directly define a sale. Instead, sales transactions that are excluded as follows: goods bought for personal, family or household use; auction sales; sales on execution or otherwise by authority of law. CISG does not directly define goods. Instead, goods that are excluded: stocks, shares, investment securities, negotiable instruments or money; ships, vessels, hovercraft or aircraft; electricity.

Part IV

Revoking Your Offer or Counter Offer

To present for sale and bid a price, when an exporter sends out information about what he is ready to sell, he gives the exact price, quality and quantity of the goods he is able to supply. This is an offer. A counter offer is a reply to an offer that adds to, limits, or modifies materially the terms of the offer, can be revoked anytime before the offeree dispatches an acceptance. (1) Subject to seller no longer being obligated to the first offer. (2) Revoke the first offer, simply say "I hereby revoked the offer." in the call. Don't get a chance to say, don't ask accepted the offer or any other question, followed up with emails, followed up with a text, sounds which record daytime but basically menu for larger offer and you're free to accept the other offer. (3) Communication of acceptance is key.

What Are Some Remedies for Breach of Contract?

Breach of contract is first of all going to be governed by what your contract says. So your contract, for example, may say that there are liquidated damages. Liquidated damages mean that if someone breaches the contract there's an absolute figure that's already been determined that is going to be the amount of the damages to be paid. This is common in a real estate transaction, for example. It may say, I'm going to keep your entire $40,000 deposit if you don't proceed with the contract. There's another thing called specific performance. Specific performance means, under certain circumstances, that the person who's breaching the contract can be forced to proceed and actually perform, make a payment, do what they're supposed to do under the contract. Actual damages can be incurred, so if I'm able to show that your breach of the contract costs me $50,000 then I can recover actual damages for the breach. And another one is injunctive relief. Injunctive relief means, let's say you and I had an agreement that you were not going to disclose my confidential information, one of which was that I was going to be filing a patent next month, and I start to see that you are out on an Internet website talking about my invention. I could go ask for an emergency injunction from the judge to stop you from doing that and to have that shut down. Those are just some of the different remedies under a breach of contract.

Part V

1. Generally, silence or inactivity does not, in and of itself, constitute acceptance. A

different result will occur, however, where a party voluntarily assumes the duty to respond, silence will constitute acceptance.

2. An international sale of goods is a sale involving parties from different countries, and a contract dealing with such a sale of transaction is a contract for the international sale of goods. There are three essential elements in an international sale of goods: Firstly, there is a sale, which is different from an exchange of goods, counter-trade of barter as a means of international commerce. Secondly, the subject matter of the sale is "goods," which has a different meaning under different laws. If a sale of goods or anything which is the subject of a sales contract is not governed by any specific domestic law or convention, the transaction will be subject to the general principles of contract law, unless the transaction is prohibited under the relevant law. Thirdly, the sale if effected at an international level, involves various international elements.

3. Withdrawal of an offer: The offeror may take an offer back before it reaches the offeree; Revocation of an offer: An offer has reached the offeree and becomes effective but before the offeree accepts it, the offeror may revoke and make it null and void.

4. An acceptance shall be in conformity with the offer. A reply with any amendments or alternation to the terms of an offer does not constitute an acceptance but a counteroffer or a new offer.

5. Fundamental Breach if defined as: When one party substantially fails to deliver what the other reasonably anticipated receiving. Avoidance Defined: The right to be excused from having to perform any obligation required by the contract. Requirements: The other party must have committed a fundamental breach; The injured party must notify the other party; The injured party must be able to return any goods he has already received.

6. The law which may affect a contract for the international sale of goods comes from three sources: international conventions; customs which have received universal recognition, such as International Chamber of Commerce (ICC) rules; and domestic laws applicable to international transactions.

Part VI
Reference:

HOLDINGS: 1. Yes. 2. Yes. 3. No. 4. No.

LAW: 1. 28 USC 1331(a) gives US district courts jurisdiction over claims that arise under "treaties of the US." 2. CISG applies when the parties are from two different CISG states. A distributor is ordinarily not an agent. 3. CISG is the law of both California and BC (because of federal supremacy rules). 4. The well-pleaded complaint rule says that a federal cause of action arises only when the plaintiff's well-pleaded complaint raises issues of federal law. The introductory text of CISG says that it is meant to establish uniform rules to promote international trade.

EXPLANATION: 1. CISG is a US treaty and therefore US district courts may hear complaints that arise under it. 2. Unique Tech. is a distributor and Asante is not bound by its actions. The transaction was thus between Asante and PMC-Sierra, both from different CISG contracting states, so the CISG applies. 3. The parties' choice of law clause adopted "California law." California law, however, includes the CISG; so the CISG is not excluded. 4. While Asante's complaint only refers to California law, the CISG is actually that law. This is because the CISG is a federal treaty that is meant to preempt all state laws. This can be seen from the CISG statement that it is meant to establish uniform international trade rules. To hold otherwise would defeat this purpose.

ORDER: Asante's motion to remand the case to state court is denied.

Lesson 22 Economic Law and Types of Property
Part II
Exercise A

1. Soviet Union, theory, system, criminal law, civil law

2. regulate, specific rules, framework, sectors

3. effects, efficient, promulgated

Answers

Exercise B

1. No.

2. In the Law of the United States and some other legal systems this approximately corresponds to the commercial law (business law).

3. The purpose of the economic law is to regulate the relations arising from the economic activities.

Part III

The Property Law

Exercise A

Chart I

Types	Features (use "√" and "×" to mark the features)
Personal property	Movable (√) Subject to ownership (√) Attached to land (×) Chattels (×)
Real property	Movable (×) Subject to ownership (×) Attached to land (√) Chattels (√)

Chart II

Tangible item (1. 3. 6. 8)	Can be touched or felt	1. Office furniture 2. Stocks
Intangible item (2. 4. 5. 7)	Cannot be touched or felt	3. Business goods 4. Bonds 5. Intellectual property 6. Business equipment 7. Money 8. Business vehicles

Exercise B

1. B

2. D

3. D

Part IV

Exercise A

1. deed

2. deed, the legal document that transfers ownership of the real property from one party to another.

3. buyer, seller, property, transferring, notarized

4. research, description, order, description

5. a warrant deed, a quitclaim deed

Exercise B

  The second type is a quitclaim deed. This type of deed transfers the ownership interest the seller has in the property, but doesn't promise, warrant or guarantee that interest. Remember that the Mulligan house has changed hands many times throughout the generations.

Lesson 23 Laws and Acts of Security

Part II

Exercise A

1. C

2. A

3. D

4. B

5. A

Exercise B

1. WWII, guaranteed, limiting

Answers

2. plaintiffs, exercising, violation, irreparable damage

Part III

Securities Act of 1933

Exercise A

1. Often referred to as the "truth in securities" law.
2. Require that investors receive financial and other significant information concerning securities being offered for public sale; and prohibit deceit, misrepresentations, and other fraud in the sale of securities.
3. In general, registration forms call for: a description of the company's properties and business; a description of the security to be offered for sale; information about the management of the company; and financial statements certified by independent accountants.
4. Self Regulatory Organizations.
5. This includes the power to register, regulate, and oversee brokerage firms, transfer agents, and clearing agencies as well as the nation's securities self regulatory organizations (SROs).

Exercise B

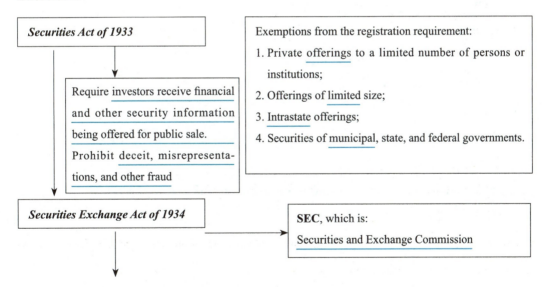

> Companies with more than $10 million in assets whose securities are held by more than 500 owners must file annual and other periodic reports.
>
> **Proxy Solicitations:** disclosure in materials used to solicit shareholders' votes in annual or special meetings
>
> **Tender Offers:** information by anyone seeking to acquire more than 5 percent of a company's securities by direct purchase or tender offer
>
> **Insider Trading:** a person trades a security while in possession of material nonpublic information in violation of a duty to withhold the information or refrain from trading.
>
> **Registration of Exchanges, Associations, and Others:** the Act requires a variety of market participants to register with the Commission, including exchanges, brokers and dealers, transfer agents, and clearing agencies.

Rule 504 of Securities

A. ☑ Government securities

☐ Bonds

☑ Foreign government securities

☐ Bank or financial institution securities

☐ Money markets

☐ CDs

☑ Insurance

☑ Public utility and railroad securities

☑ Non-profit securities

☑ Employee benefit plans

B. A B C

Lesson 24 Business Law: Consumer Protection and Product Liability
Part II

1. American culture places a high value on material possessions and encourages people to consume more than they need.

2. Consumer Protection.

3. The FTC protects these rights by: Enforcing product, safety distributing, consumer-related information, preventing deceptive marketing.

Answers

4. Product liability.

5. Product liability laws are state laws.

6. Design flaws. Manufacturing defects. A failure to warn consumers of a possible danger.

Part III

Consumer Protection Legislation in EU

Exercise A

1. ☐ The Charter of Fundamental Rights

   ☐ The Directive on Consumer Rights

   ☑ The Federal Trade Commission

   ☐ The guidance document

2. D

3. D

4. C

5. C

Exercise B

The Charter of Fundamental Rights and the European treaties since the Single European Act guarantee a high level of consumer protection in the EU. It is also a general objective defined in Article 12 of the Treaty on the Functioning of the EU. European legislation guarantees consumers: fair treatment; products which meet acceptable standards; a right of redress if something goes wrong. EU legislation in other areas also has to take consumer protection into account.

Unfair or Deceptive Trade Practices

Exercise A

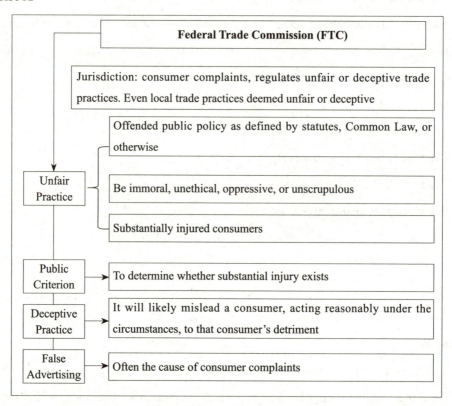

Exercise B

1. A
2. D
3. G
4. B
5. E
6. F
7. C

Lesson 25 Law of Contract (1) : Basic Principles

Part II

Exercise A

1. A
2. G
3. B
4. C
5. H
6. F
7. D
8. E
9. I

Part III

Basic Principles of the Law of Contract

Exercise A

Contract: formation		
offer	**acceptance**	**consideration**
It may include simplistic or complex terms, but it must be concrete and affirmed through written documentation.	One part will affirmatively accept the offer; the original offer may be accepted in a written or spoken form.	Consideration can take the form of refraining from performing a function or doing something that the party is otherwise entitled to initiate.

*Offer + acceptance = mutual assent

Mutual assent + consideration = contract

Exercise B

1. The law of contract states that the first step required to form a valid contract is that an offer must be formally made by one of the parties to another.
2. The purchaser must make an offer to purchase the underlying property.

3. Following the offer, the contract, as stated by the law of contract, must be accepted by the offered party.

4. If the offered party proposes a counteroffer, an acceptance is not realized.

5. To be given for the contract to maintain a legal or valid status.

6. Money, assets, and so on.

Capacity in Contract Law—Minor

Exercise A

1. minors, intoxication, mental incompetence

2. Minors

3. Service, training, apprenticeship

4. Defective, beneficial

5. Force, personal service, public policy, forced, will

Exercise B

1. He is not bound by the contract.

2. Contracts that are considered for the benefit of the minor are that of service, education, training, apprenticeship and employment. However, the courts will reject a contract if it is considered not in the benefit of a minor. The contract had conditions which were considered not beneficial to the minor and therefore, the minor was not bound by the contact.

Part V

Exercise A

1. A. specifically details exactly what will be provided

   B. the agreement by the other party to the offer presented

   C. money or something of interest being exchanged between the parties

   D. age and mental ability

   E. carry out their promise

   F. object of the contract

2. A. a lease

   B. down payment

   C. key

   express

Exercise B

An unambiguous offer and acceptance. Mutuality of both parties to be bound to the contract. Consideration.

Lesson 26 Law of Contract (2) : Breach and Remedies
Part II
Definition: Breach of Contract
Exercise B

Breach of Contract
Legal sense: failure to fulfill contractual obligations
Categories: material and immaterial (minor)
Aspect: (civil law or criminal law?) civil law
Legal solution: remedy
Common law: damages
Equity law: rescission, restitution, specific performance, injunction, and so on.

Exercise C

Factors that the courts consider in determining materiality
1. The amount of benefit received by the non-breaching party;
2. Whether the non-breaching party can be adequately compensated for the damages;
3. The extent of performance by the breaching party;
4. Hardship to the breaching party;
5. Negligent or willful behavior of the breaching party; and
6. The likelihood that the breaching party will perform the remainder of the contract.

Exercise D

2. 1. 3. 5. 4.

Exercise E

1. T

2. F

3. F

4. T

5. F

Breach of Contract

Exercise A

1. formalize

2. sompensation

3. immaterial

4. significant, central, goal

5. remedied, wronged, obligations

Exercise B

Often, one party to a contract fails to uphold his or her obligations under the contract. This results in a breach of contract. Because contracts are legally binding, a breach of contract results in legal consequences. Once a court decides that a breach has occurred, it will issue a remedy.

Part III

Correct: 2. 4.

Lesson 27 Antitrust Law and Sherman Act

Part II

Exercise A

1. Google.

2. EU may consider it has strong case otherwise they won't file the case.

3. A lot of critics believe EU is putting on protectionism.

4. Microsoft.

5. Abuse of market dominant position.

Answers

Exercise B

Which processes will the company go through, according to the interview? Click the possible ones.

- ☑ Respondent letter
- ☑ Hearing
- ☑ Defense actions
- ☐ Counterclaim
- ☐ Complaint
- ☐ Discrimination
- ☑ Settlement

Part III

Antitrust Law

Antitrust law is a set of statutes developed to regulate competition between companies, mainly to ensure that businesses are engaging in fair competition.

Purpose: to protect consumers from greedy business owners

Since 1800s, government intervened unfair practices

Forms of unfair competition

Monopoly: refers to a total market share taken by one single company, making it impossible for other competitors to make a fair buck.

Market allocation: refers to two companies conspiring to divide a market in order for two businesses to sell similar products at higher prices to drive away competition.

Bid rigging: refers to two or more companies agree to price bids unfairly.

Price fixing: refers to two companies set higher than average prices for a product that is only available for purchase by the two companies.

Trusts and Monopolies

Exercise A

1. C

2. B

3. D

4. C

Exercise B

Economists believe that such control injures both individuals and the public because it leads to anticompetitive practices in an effort to obtain or maintain total control. Anticompetitive practices then lead to price controls and diminished individual initiative. These results in turn cause markets to stagnate and depress economic growth.

Lesson 28 Types and Laws of Competition

Part II

Exercise A

Product

Place

Promotion

Price

Exercise B

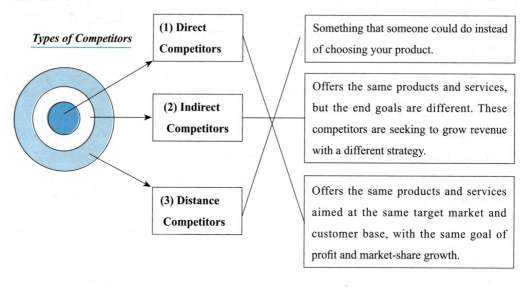

Part III

1. AT&T.
2. AT&T controlled the long-distance telephone service, most local telephone service, and a substantial amount of all telephone equipment manufacturing. The decree split AT&T from its local telephone service subsidiaries.
3. Because it involved in stopping new competition in long-distance service.
4. First, it creates a legal method through which local telephone service companies may enter long-distance markets, and in setting forth the second alternative, the Act recognizes that actual local competition might not prove practical.
5. The judge agrees with the Court's disposition of the FCC's "unbundling" rules.

Part IV

Exercise A

1. It can refer only to those torts involving an attempt to pass off goods or services as if they belonged to another business, and also other kinds of misbehaviors.
2. [Logo] She even used the same pink logo.

   [Marketing list] She steals the client list.

   [Trade secrets] Wilma misappropriated the trade secrets when she left.

   [Advertisement] The same and alike memo is used.

   [Price] Much lower.
3. A trade secret is any confidential business information that provides the business with a competitive edge. This includes things like sales methods, distribution methods, marketing methods, research methods, consumer profiles, advertising strategies, suppliers lists, client lists, firm software, and manufacturing processes.

Lesson 29 Criminal Law (1): Basic Principles
Part II
Definitions and Differences
Exercise A

1. C

2. E

3. B

4. C D

Exercise B

A cause of action is the legal basis, or claim, allowing one party to seek a court judgment against another.

Exercise C

A prosecution is simply a legal cause of action in which someone is charged with a crime. Generally speaking, crimes are wrongs for which the government prescribes a legal punishment.

News Report
Exercise A

1. President Barack Obama is calling for major changes to the American criminal justice system.

2. African-Americans, Latinos, non-violent

3. action, reform, drug crack-cocaine, minimum, higher

Settlement

1. dropped

2. retained

3. enforce

4. breached, initiate, intervention

5. liability, contempt

Lesson 30 Criminal Law (2): Plea Bargaining and Cross Examination
Part II
Arraignment

1. In County Court Criminal Division.

2. To make clear about the rights and the consequences.

3. If I plea guilty, I am admitting charges against myself.

4. silent, considered, jury, attorney, attorney, jail sentence

5. testify, witnesses, proceedings, appeal, error

Opening Statement

1. The Judge.

2. I will face a fine, a jail sentence or both.

3. Yes.

4. Yes, I will plea guilty, because otherwise I will face a trial and have to return to court. Once I have pleaded guilty, as my violation is not very serious, I may just face a fine.

5. No, I can't. Only when the state is seeking jail time against me in the event that I am found guilty and I do not have adequate funds can I hire my own lawyer.

About the Plea Bargaining

1. T
2. T
3. T
4. T
5. F

Part IV

1. F
2. T
3. T
4. T

Boston Legal

1. Because the attorney's question seemed off the subject and too easy as a common sense.
2. It is obvious, but the attorney wanted to prove that the witness was not possible to confirm the defendants in such conditions.
3. At last the witness was not sure about whether the defendants were present at the scene or it was other people, which was useful and helpful for the attorney.
4. a. to diminish the harmful effect of the witness's direct testimony

   b. to reduce the credibility of the witness

   c. to obtain information that is helpful to the cross-examiner's side

Badgering the Witness

1. "Badgering the witness" is the proper objection for a lawyer who is antagonizing or mocking a witness by asking insulting or derisive questions, perhaps in an attempt to provoke an emotional response.
2. I can make objections and in hope of that the judge will sustain my objection.
3. She was provoked by the opposing attorney, and cursed him in the court.